About Demos

Demos is a greenhouse for new ideas which can improve the quality of our lives. As an independent think tank, we aim to create an open resource of knowledge and learning that operates beyond traditional party politics.

We connect researchers, thinkers and practitioners to an international network of people changing politics. Our ideas regularly influence government policy, but we also work with companies, NGOs, colleges and professional bodies.

Demos knowledge is organised around five themes, which combine to create new perspectives. The themes are democracy, learning, enterprise, quality of life and global change.

But we also understand that thinking by itself is not enough. Demos has helped to initiate a number of practical projects which are delivering real social benefit through the redesign of public services.

We bring together people from a wide range of backgrounds to cross-fertilise ideas and experience. By working with Demos, our partners develop a sharper insight into the way ideas shape society. For Demos, the process is as important as the final product.

www.demos.co.uk

First published in 2004
© Demos
Some rights reserved – see copyright licence for details

ISBN 1 84180 120 8
Typeset by Land & Unwin, Bugbrooke
Printed by Hendy Banks, London

For further information and
subscription details please contact:

Demos
The Mezzanine
Elizabeth House
39 York Road
London SE1 7NQ

telephone: 020 7401 5330
email: hello@demos.co.uk
web: www.demos.co.uk

Free For All?

Public service television in the digital age

Barry Cox

DEMCS

Contents

Acknowledgements

This booklet is based on a series of four lectures I gave in Oxford early in 2003 as that year's News International Visiting Professor of Broadcast Media at the University. I am very grateful to the organising committee, and its chair, the Rector of Exeter College, Professor Marilyn Butler, for giving me the opportunity to hold forth at such length. My particular thanks go to two committee members, Paddy Coulter and Gillian Reynolds, for the support and fellowship they provided during the preparation and delivery of these lectures.

I must also thank those who read and commented on various drafts, in part or in whole: Clive Ansell, Andy Barnes, Sir Alan Budd, Mick Desmond, Robin Foster, Peter Ibbotson, John Newbigin, David Scott, Mark Thompson and Gary Tonge. Thanks also to Beverley Kotey for her help with the research, and to Danuta Miloszewski for producing the typescripts.

Two people in particular gave generously of their time and intellectual effort: Julian Dickens and Tim Gardam. They corrected errors and subjected the arguments to penetrating criticism well beyond the calls of either friendship or duty, and I am very grateful to both of them.

My wife Fiona not only read and commented on everything: she rehearsed me rigorously so that the Oxford audiences might have a chance of comprehending what I was on about. If I succeeded, it is very much down to her.

That a wider audience was exposed to these ideas is the result of the support of two people: Georgina Henry, the deputy editor of the *Guardian*, who read the drafts and got the lectures the best possible send-off by giving me space to summarise them in the Media Guardian (along with an eye-catching front cover); and Richard Tait, who used them as the basis for two insightful columns in the Creative Business section of the *Financial Times*. I am very grateful to both of them, the more so as they didn't agree with my views on the BBC.

A year later, and Demos has decided that the ideas are still pertinent – perhaps even more so – and has given me the chance to amend, edit and update the material into the form in which you now see it – along with adding a chapter on the BBC Charter Review issues. My thanks to Tom Bentley and Eddie Gibb for this opportunity; to Nader Mazhar for additional research; and special thanks to David Lee for his help in updating the material, and in particular for contributing the 'open source' ideas.

Finally I should emphasise that these are personal views and not those of either Channel 4 or the Digital TV Stakeholders Group.

Executive summary

We should take advantage of the arrival of digital to create the kind of conventional market in television programmes that we have never hitherto been able to have. For the BBC, this mean a choice between continuing as a large organisation funded through voluntary means, or continuing as a scaled-down publicly funded broadcaster. To do this, three fundamental features of the current broadcasting world need changing, features that can be expressed thus:

O   the problem with free television is that none of us pays for it directly
O   the problem with the BBC is that we pay for it whether we want it or not
O   the problem with digital television is that we cannot just pay for what we want.

This means breaking two powerful monopolies, which is now made possible through use of digital technologies. Those two broadcasting monopolies are:

O   the BBC, which has exclusive use of the licence fee
O   Sky, which takes two-thirds of all pay TV revenues.

Digital TV and paid-for services

Neither ITV nor Channel 4 are likely to be able to perform their traditional public service roles in the digital era. Many free channels –

that is those funded by advertising – will become vehicles for the promotion of the wider commercial interests of their owners.

To bring about a conventional market where TV programmes are financed by a mix of pay and advertising, Ofcom must ensure that dominant platform operators like Sky allow people to buy only those channels that they actually want.

The BBC and Channel 4 should remain public corporations, with obligations to provide high-quality news and current affairs services, and with some compensatory privileges; but they should be free to choose the rest of their programme services, and free to choose how they mix advertising and pay TV revenues. They should, like other broadcasters and programme producers, be able to obtain public money for certain kinds of programmes or services that are not commercially viable. Although the government is not going to abolish the BBC licence fee in its current review of the BBC Charter, it can prepare the way for a new broadcast environment.

Three technologies now in their infancy will affect the broadcast market once they are in widespread use. These 'disruptive technologies' are:

O   wired and wireless broadband services
O   personal video recorders
O   micro-billing payment systems.

The switch over from analogue to digital television is one of the key elements in enabling a conventional television market to emerge. As a result, the UK has a greater percentage of digital households – around 50 per cent – than any other country. Within ten years it is highly probable we will have gone fully digital.

Free TV

Free television funded entirely by advertising will continue to be available as the equivalent of newspaper freesheets today. The basic nature of free television – that it is a promotional tool for commerce – is being exposed in an ever-increasing variety of ways. One recent long-term advertising expenditure forecast suggested that television's share of advertising expenditure could drop from the 27.9 per cent it took in 2001 to 24.5 per cent in 2014.

Nearly half the country has shown it is willing to pay more than £300 a year per household – on top of the £116 licence fee – to get extra TV channels and services: yet most of the programmes viewers get for that money are watched less than those they get for free. Programme sponsorship and advertising are still carefully regulated on the main terrestrial channels, though these rules are being periodically revised and relaxed as the financial pressures on the traditional broadcasters increase.

The main trends affecting our existing broadcast model are:

○ Overall advertising expenditure could decline.

○ ITV's share of TV audiences and advertising has been falling steadily for several years, though Channel 4's share of both has until this year been stable; the pressure on both networks to maximise revenues from each programme will intensify.

○ Costs of original production and acquired material are rising, making public service commitments harder to keep.

○ New digital revenue opportunities will tempt broadcasters to regard their programme schedules as both a direct and indirect way of getting viewers to spend money on products and services in which the broadcaster has a direct commercial stake.

ITV

There is real ongoing value in allowing separate companies in Ulster, Scotland and the Channel Islands, even though there is now one big English company.

A profound reform would be to allow the ITV companies to charge viewers to watch some of their programmes if they wanted to – and this is still not permitted in the Communications Act.

The ITV network should continue to provide some kind of public service broadcasting in return for its privileged position, at least until we switch from analogue to digital broadcasting. Expectations of the public service contribution the network can make should be limited to:

○   a quality news service
○   a high level of original production
○   a limited regional service.

BSkyB

BSkyB exploited control of content (movies and sport) and technology (satellite broadcasting) to create an attractive retail package that made it difficult for competitors to emerge. As a result there has been no effective competition either within the UK satellite market, nor between different pay TV operators, particularly in the provision of alternative film and sports channels. Subscribers have no alternative choice, while BSkyB prevents them for paying for what they watch – sport and movies – and they have to subscribe to a basic package, which contains channels people don't watch. The government took the view that only by allowing big companies to reap the rewards of a monopoly would they invest in new technologies. However, BSkyB is now close to paying off its debt and this argument no longer holds.

UK governments and regulators have been able to dodge many of the hard decisions about competition in digital television, and our expanding pay TV market continues to be dominated by a single vertically integrated operator. Ofcom should take a stronger line with BSkyB than the Office of Fair Trading managed. Its objective should be to create a conventional market where people can freely choose what they want to spend their money on. Ofcom should consider:

○   the unbundling and buy-through practices that the Independent Television Commission left in place when it renewed them in 1998 o   regulating the pricing structures of pay TV, so that the platform operators cannot solely determine the price at which channels and individual programmes are sold.

The BBC and Charter Review

The problem with the BBC is that we have to pay for it, whether we want it or not. The context in which our public service broadcasters operate has changed – and will continue to change – so profoundly that we will have to rethink what we mean by public service broadcasting.

The government review of the BBC Charter, together with the review of all public service broadcasting that Ofcom is required to carry out in 2004, offers an excellent opportunity to start serious thinking now. There are three public service objectives that need to be addressed in the free-market digital world. They are:

o   to ensure that there are at least two competing high-quality, impartial news and current affairs services freely available

o   to guarantee subsidies to ensure that certain kinds of culturally and educationally valuable programmes or services can be made available either for free or at an affordable price

o   to provide subsidies to make sure that those who live in remote areas have access to a minimum number of digital services.

We are approaching that 'near-perfect' market in television. In such circumstances the argument put by the Peacock Committee nearly 20 years ago for the abolition of the licence fee and its replacement by subscription seems overwhelming. Public service ethos, which includes ITV and Channel 4, is being undermined by the new, commercial values that dominate the creative culture in contemporary television. It is highly probable that the current funding system, of a compulsory licence fee, will run until the end of 2016. By that time Britain will almost certainly be well into the digital era.

Possible outcomes for this review process are:

○ *Top-slicing*
The BBC would no longer be the sole beneficiary of the licence fee, with the creation of a 'contestable fund', which producers could bid for to make public service programmes.

○ *Reform of BBC governors*
Options include putting the BBC fully under Ofcom, and turning the governors into non-executive board members (or retaining the governors as a regulatory body but separated from the BBC, with its own staff and resources).

○ *Tighter channel remits*
The government is likely to insist that BBC1 and BBC2 have more tightly defined remits, which set out their public service commitments in more detail.

○ *Open source*
Following former director-general Greg Dyke's recent announcement about putting its programme archive online, the BBC could position itself as an 'open source' producer committed to creating a national cultural asset.

1. Introduction

In Britain we have been fortunate in our experience of television. For the past 50 years it has provided a wonderful creative environment for many of our best writers, performers, directors and journalists – more so, probably, than in any other country. It could continue to do this, perhaps for another 50 years – even though television in the digital era will not be television as we know it now.

However, to achieve this outcome we must recognise the revolutionary implications for our current broadcast structure of what is an uninteresting truism in most other areas of life: you get what you pay for. We need, in short, to transform ourselves from passive viewers into active consumers.

To do this, three fundamental features of the current broadcasting world need changing, features that can be expressed thus:

O   the problem with free television is that none of us pays for it directly
O   the problem with the BBC is that we pay for it whether we want it or not
O   the problem with digital television is that we cannot just pay for what we want.

The way to remove these market barriers is simple to describe, though seriously difficult to achieve, given the power of the biggest beneficiaries of today's arrangements – the BBC and Sky – to prevent it. *We should take advantage of the arrival of digital to create the kind of conventional market in television programmes that we have never hitherto been able to have.*

In the digital world all broadcasters and producers should be free to choose how they get their programmes to us, and we should be free to choose how we want to receive them – in particular how we want to pay for them. This means breaking two powerful monopolies. The BBC has exclusive use of the licence fee, and Sky takes two-thirds of all pay TV revenues. Digital technologies, if we make full use of them, allow us to do away with these monopolies.

But we will also have to give up the idea of providing a wide range of high-quality broadcasting to everybody free at the point of use. And this is the core difficulty with the communications revolution – it is bound to be socially divisive for some years. Some of those who might benefit most from the arrival of digital may well be unable – or unwilling – to acquire the technology. Some will argue that giving up our current system of public service broadcasting and expecting everyone to pay for most of their TV viewing would exacerbate this divide. But doing nothing will sharpen it anyway. What we as individual consumers spend on TV is growing faster than what the advertisers spend, and the balance between pay and free will continue to shift in favour of paid for TV.

In 2002 we spent £4.0 billion on the BBC licence fee (TV) and pay TV subscriptions, compared with the £3.1 billion spent by advertisers.[1] In 2003 the old Independent Television Commission forecast that by 2012 pay TV revenues would reach £8.5 billion a year, as against £4.6 billion from advertising. This is ignoring the billions we also spend on DVDs, videos and video games – many of which we use via the TV screen.

It is far better in my view to recognise this reality, and find ways to maximise the potential benefits from this trend, while at the same time revising the policies with which we currently try to deal with the social and cultural issues that we rightly believe are necessary for the media.

So what in such a world happens to people who can't afford to pay for their TV programmes? Well, it is possible to argue that people have no more right to free TV services than they do to, say, free transport – and in Britain we only provide that on a very limited basis. People over age 75 don't have to pay a TV licence fee, and pensioners get a free bus pass, but not a free car. However, I recognise that even in the digital world we will need significant public intervention in the market.

Given that there are bound to be some free TV channels, even in the digital world, what exactly will we need to subsidise through public support? I think there will be three different kinds of market failure, which will need different kinds of remedies and different kinds of public funding.

Different kinds of market failure

The first is geographical. Both British Telecom (BT) and the public service broadcasters currently have to make sure that their networks reach almost everyone in the country, even though the cost of doing this for at least one million households in remote areas makes little commercial sense now, and may make even less in the digital and broadband future.

At the moment BT, the BBC, ITV and Channel 4 can be expected to carry this universal service obligation because they have been the beneficiaries of long-standing historic monopolies. Since these monopolies have either gone (in the case of ITV and Channel 4), are going (BT) or ought to go (the BBC) in the digital world, we will eventually need to find another way of meeting the geographic problems. One obvious way would be to fund through taxation the parts of the telecoms and broadcasting networks that fail the commercial test.

The second is a civic problem. We want the citizens of our democracy to have a decent chance of knowing what is going on in the world, if only to make an informed decision when it comes to electing governments. We will continue to want everyone to have access to a range of broadcast journalistic services, and we will not want these only to come from a handful of commercial operators who for reasons of their own are prepared to provide them free – though there certainly will be some such companies.

It is largely so that they can continue to provide without charge high-quality, impartial, fair and accurate news and current affairs (both national and international) that I think the BBC and Channel 4 should remain public corporations in the digital age. As public corporations their news services can be overseen by Ofcom, to ensure the delivery of all these characteristics, which may or may not be available from purely commercial companies. (There are already moves by some commercial broadcasters to offer more opinionated and partisan news services.) If we consider what the unregulated provision of news has led to in our newspapers, we would be prudent to be cautious about sweeping away all content regulation in broadcasting.

If we do, as I hope, in due course abolish the licence fee, we will need to offer these public corporations some privileges in return for undertaking this relatively expensive obligation. These could take the form of subsidised access to the distribution networks, of relief from the charges for use of the terrestrial spectrum that commercial businesses will have to pay the government, or prominent displays on all programme guides – or some mix of these.

The third and final form of market failure is likely to be cultural – that programmes and services that we would like to be available to all might only be provided to those who could afford them, or not even provided at all. Traditionally this list has included arts, religion, original (and non-cartoon) children's programmes, documentaries, education, social action and minority appeal drama. Again, we can argue about the exact content of such a list, but I suspect future governments will always want to see some of these features provided as a public service.

We could of course insist that this should be the job – and the only job – of the BBC, and expect it to do it with fewer channels than now and with a much reduced licence fee (since it wouldn't need to do all that popular stuff it does now). The BBC has always resisted this, on the grounds that if everyone pays the licence fee then everyone should find something they want on its screens – not just the programmes other broadcasters don't want to make. Yet this approach is scarcely an answer to the market failure problem, as many commentators have pointed out over the years.

In my view there are better reasons for rejecting this 'ghetto BBC' approach. There are real benefits from having a big, wide-ranging BBC. It is a great broadcaster, which knows how to make a very wide range of programmes very well. It would be crazy not to try to retain this national asset. At the same time we need diversity and competition in the provision of minority appeal services as much as in more popular ones. Putting all our subsidy money into one ghetto broadcaster, a greatly diminished and restricted BBC, would be a bad mistake on both counts.

The answer that the Peacock Committee gave nearly 20 years ago was to create a broadcasting equivalent of the Arts Council, which would use public money to fund such programmes from a range of sources and across a range of broadcasters and platforms.[2] It is an idea that is periodically revived, and periodically secures some support. It has been adopted in New Zealand and Singapore (though not entirely successfully in New Zealand's case). We actually follow this policy in a modest way in Britain already, with the funding of Gaelic broadcasting in Scotland. And this, or something like it, will surely be the mechanism we will end up using on a much larger scale at some point in the digital era.

Summary

Free television is changing, probably fundamentally. Neither ITV nor Channel 4 are likely to be able to perform their traditional public service roles in the digital era. Many free channels – that is those funded by advertising – will become vehicles for the promotion of the wider commercial interests of their owners. Nothing wrong with that, but it is not the ideal environment for public service broadcasting (see chapter 3).

It will be better for us as a society and as individuals if we expect to pay for our use of television, much in the way we pay for most goods and services. To bring about a conventional market where TV programmes are financed by a mix of pay and advertising, we need the new regulator, Ofcom – perhaps supported by new legislation – to encourage, even force, dominant platform operators like Sky to allow people to buy only those channels that they actually want, not a compulsory mix of basic and premium services, as now happens (see chapter 5).

In this kind of conventional market, the justification for a licence fee-funded BBC disappears – as Gavyn Davies, the former BBC chairman who resigned following the publication of the Hutton report, acknowledged in 1999.[3] At the same time the programme-making culture is becoming more motivated by the desire to make money, and less by the desire to make the world a better place. These two developments demand a major reformation of the BBC (see chapter 6).

So in the digital era we will need radically different public service arrangements. The BBC and Channel 4 should remain public corporations, with obligations to provide high-quality news and current affairs services, and with some compensatory privileges, but free to choose the rest of their programme services, and free to choose how they mix advertising and pay TV revenues. They should, like other broadcasters and programme producers, be able to obtain public money for certain kinds of programmes or services that are not commercially viable. The government may also need to fund the delivery of some services to remote parts of the country that no commercial business could be expected to reach unaided. Such radical reforms will not happen easily.

All this is both possible and, in my view, desirable – once we live in a fully digital world. But that is probably ten years away. In the meantime the government has to decide what to do about the BBC Charter, due for renewal in 2006.

It is not going to abolish the licence fee this time round (and nor should it). However, it could make a number of changes, some of which could prepare the way for a new broadcast environment and new kind of public service provision better than others. These potential outcomes form the matter of chapter 7.

2. The potential of disruptive technologies

This booklet addresses the profound reshaping of the world of broadcasting that could be brought about by a decade of techno-logical and market-driven change, combined with innovation by service providers, political and regulatory decision-making. Key to this subject are three disruptive technologies. Now in their infancy, they will be in widespread use within a decade:

○ wired and wireless broadband services
○ personal video recorders
○ micro-billing payment systems.

This combination of technologies will enable us – if we want it – to move to a conventional marketplace for the purchase and consumption of what, as a shorthand, I will continue to call television programmes, though the products and services widely available by then will go way beyond what we currently think of as TV programmes.

This may sound like one more example of nerdy, techno-visionary guff. However, after some 20 years of listening to such prophecies and then seeing them fail to happen, I do believe that we have now crossed a watershed. Not only are the relevant technologies now up and running in people's homes – albeit in a small minority of homes at the moment – but we have had a decade of evidence of what the introduction of pay television services does to the traditional broadcast environment. We have also seen the growth of vigorous competitors for the use of the TV set – most notably video games, videos and DVDs. And with the Communications Act we have a major change in public policy towards that environment. Put all these together and we have the potential for a fundamental transformation in the way television is produced, distributed and consumed.

For shorthand convenience I have generally referred to 'television programmes' and 'channels'. In fact a significant amount of what we will be using our television screens for in 2014 will not be television as we know it. Half the country already uses the internet for a range of activities and transactions (though this is largely through PCs and mobile handsets, rather than TV screens at the moment). The range of experiences available from these new technologies will continue to grow. These user technologies will be increasingly integrated with faster distribution systems, both wired and wireless. It is this combination that I believe can turn most homes into electronic retail outlets.

In an important sense the technologies are not the issue. Their capabilities and potential are already sufficiently understood. It is the economics that will determine what we actually have in our homes and how we use it, together with the business models adopted by the most important companies, and the effectiveness of the competition regime under which they operate. And it is governments that will have to decide how to deal with the social and cultural consequences of these developments.

Digital television

First, there is the switch over from analogue to digital television, one of the key elements in enabling a conventional television market to emerge.

Government, broadcasters and manufacturers are keen to make this switch for a number of reasons. Digital is a much more efficient transmission mechanism than analogue, and a digital receiver can do much more than an analogue one can. The benefits to the economy, to particular businesses, and to the consumers – once they can be persuaded to adopt digital – are considerable. So since the 1990s broadcasters have been investing in digital transmissions and, in many cases, subsidising receiver equipment. As a result the UK has a greater percentage of digital households – around 50 per cent – than any other country.[4]

The government has said that it would like to see the entire country switch to digital television at some point between 2006 and 2010. However, it won't allow the terrestrial broadcasters to switch off their analogue transmissions until digital reception is available to 99 per cent of the country, and until it is clear that the digital receivers are affordable for everyone.

The first test has already been achieved. Digital terrestrial, cable and satellite, taken together, cover nearly all the country, but that is largely down to the signals from the Luxemburg Astra satellite used by Sky. At the moment the terrestrial network built so far can reach around three-quarters of households in this country. However, the BBC, ITV and Channel 4 are considering replicating the current analogue network of 1,150 transmitters in full, which would enable them to reach 99 per cent of the country. During 2003 a range of digital adapters that can be connected to analogue sets arrived on the market. These have been selling well at prices from around £40 to £150. It is quite likely – indeed it happens already – that people buying other equipment – flatscreen, widescreen sets, DVD players and so on – will get an adaptor thrown in free. The government hasn't said whether these developments mean we now pass the affordability test. It is planning a consultation on when we should switch off the analogue signal later this year (2004).

It will take at least two years to start switching off analogue and at least another four to complete the terrestrial digital network once the government has agreed its final shape with the public service broadcasters. The earliest that switchover could start is 2007 and it is likely to happen one region at a time. So, even allowing for slippage, it is highly probable we will have gone fully digital by 2014.

Personal video recorders

The second of the technologies that I have highlighted as crucial to the market revolution I am advocating, personal video recorders (PVRs), are important because – with their capacity to store and organise many hours of recorded material – they provide the shelving in the electronic home bookshop.

PVRs are already being marketed in Britain. The most successful is Sky-Plus, with a built-in hard disk drive. In its first year it had 120,000 subscribers.[5] The evidence is that once people have learned how to use PVRs they value them very highly indeed; PVRs transform their viewing habits – almost everything is watched through the PVR rather than live. Manufacturers like PACE and Philips are proposing to bring terrestrial free-to-air PVRs to market later this year.

Broadband

The other key technology is broadband. This comes in various forms: down the copper telephone line from BT by Digital Subscriber Line (DSL); through optic fibre cables from ntl and Telewest; and over the air, from satellite and other wireless transmissions. Broadband has been slower to develop in the UK than in some other countries, but since a change in policy at BT in 2002 new broadband products have been on offer at a reasonable price. Backed by a substantial promotional campaign, things speeded up considerably. We now have more than three million broadband subscribers (including those with cable)[6] and BT forecasts that it alone will have five million DSL customers by the middle of 2006.[7]

Needless to say there are difficulties with the roll-out of broadband, geography and economics being the dominant ones. Even with improvements to the current technologies it is thought unlikely that more than 90 per cent of the country can be connected, commercially, in the next ten years – though recently BT suggested it could be done in partnership with local authorities which were able to offer some knd of subsidy.

It is also true that the word broadband covers distribution technologies with a wide range of capabilities. DSL in the UK from BT, for example, is about ten times faster than the standard dial-up internet modem; ntl and Telewest will provide capacity between four times and 20 times faster, depending on how much you are willing to pay. (In Germany it can be up to 30 times faster.) These capabilities are improving steadily, and are expected to continue to improve for some years yet. I am confident that the electronic motorways of the future, both wired and wireless, can carry enough traffic to stock the electronic homes of Britain with a wide range of products and services.

How many of us will be able and willing to afford these services, and how businesses will make money out of providing them, is more problematic. At the moment one of the few applications that is keenly welcomed by a particular group of consumers is playing games online. The other favourite use is to swap audio and video files. If you have paid to be 'always on', it doesn't matter much to you if it takes several hours overnight to download a two-hour film for free from the internet. This is of course strictly theft of the film studio's property, and a breach of their copyright.

This problem will get worse as broadband is rolled out more widely, and as compression techniques reduce the time taken to download material. A digital copy is a perfect copy, and can be acquired and redistributed in perfect form. Content owners are understandably getting very agitated, and trying to find ways of preventing widespread piracy. The US Congress has passed legislation that makes it a criminal offence to distribute software that enables such activities.

People on the telecoms side of the industry say that the Hollywood studios, the music companies and other content owners have got it wrong. Neither law nor technology can or should stop broadband being used to distribute audio and video products. Instead, the content owners should adapt their own distribution processes to make their films, programmes and so on available for a price. Their argument is that while the nerds and hackers might enjoy using their time and energies to bypass sensible procedures, most of us will be happy to behave lawfully if we are enabled to do so conveniently and at a reasonable price. Since the cable and telecoms companies already have effective micro-payment systems in place – the regular telephone bill – they could administer such processes easily.

As ever we in Britain are a couple of years behind the US, but government and industry are beginning to address these issues in detail. I suspect that the outcome will be a pragmatic mix of all the solutions currently being advocated: technological barriers to unauthorised use, legislation outlawing certain activities, new business models that accept broadband distribution and rely on the current billing systems for payments, and a reluctant toleration of a certain amount of hacking and piracy.

There are already some interesting uses of broadband. The Department of Health is rolling out a digital service based on a number of pilot experiments like one conducted by Telewest in Birmingham. It was called Living Health, and available to their 36,000 broadband subscribers in that city.[8] One of the most fascinating features was the way it enabled people to contact NHS Direct. The nurse on duty had a video camera linked to her broadband connec-tion, so that patients could have a direct conversation with a visible human being. This was understandably popular with both the nurses and their patients. Interestingly, the two groups that used it most were the two groups that are least willing to visit their GPs – young and old men. There are other kinds of counselling and advice services – Citizens' Advice Bureaux, for example, or MPs' constituency surgeries – that could well benefit from this use of the new technologies.

A possible future

So, how will the vision of the electronic home bookshop of the digital future work? It is probably easiest to start with a print analogy that exists right now. One TV colleague of mine has given up buying the Sunday newspapers. Every day he gets emailed to his home a summary of the main stories in the day's papers, provided by an agency. On Sundays he looks at the summary, and if he sees a story he wants to read in full, he goes to the newspaper website and reads it there. It saves him time and money, and he hasn't got a small forest of newsprint in his house to plough through.

Translate that practice to the world of film, television and video in the digital broadband age, and see how it ought to work. Let's say you subscribe to 20 channels, half of them premium standalone services, the rest a bundle of cheaper channels that you buy en bloc. Your PVR has automatic access to these, plus all the free advertising-funded channels. Before you go to work you tell it the two films or programmes you want it to record. It might, of its own accord, also record a couple of hours of other programmes it thinks you will like.

When you get back in the evening you choose one of the recorded shows to watch. In addition, you have heard at work about – and read newspaper reviews of – a programme on a channel you don't subscribe to that went out the day before and that sounds very interesting. You go to the relevant website – it could be the broadcaster's, it could belong to the programme producer, or it could be a video-on-demand service – and order it to be downloaded so you can watch it when convenient. You will pay for it in your next bill from the telephone or cable company.

The next day you realise there was something on one of the free channels that you missed, but fortunately your PVR did spot it and recorded it for you. You choose to watch it with the adverts cut out – so you will be charged for this at the end of the month.

There are all kinds of variations on that model, but I trust you get the idea. It is what the combination of personal video recorders, broadband distribution and micro-payment systems can do. But it requires significant changes to our current TV business models. The most important change is that every TV channel (including those from the BBC) should be able to choose how it was funded – by advertising, by subscription or by single viewing payments, or any combination of these. This means changing the BBC Charter, scrapping the current legislative rules that prevent ITV and Channel 4 charging for their programmes, and obliging the pay TV retailers – Sky, the cable and telecoms companies – to share their revenues with their suppliers equitably.

At the same time viewers should be free to pay for what they want – which means abolishing the licence fee for television (though not perhaps for radio), preventing cable and satellite operators from forcing customers to buy basic channels in order to receive premium ones, and limiting their ability to bundle channels into packages.

Electronic retail outlet versus twin supermarkets

The difficult question is whether we – or more precisely our politicians and regulators – will manage this transformation in a way that delivers a good or bad outcome. As of now I regret to say that a bad outcome is just as likely as a good one.

The good outcome is simple to describe. Our homes can become an electronic retail outlet, the equivalent of a video version of WH Smith. Something similar to the range of diverse print products available to us now – newspapers, magazines, books – in a decent-sized branch of WH Smith could be available electronically (though of course this domestic electronic store would offer stuff, for example online gaming and gambling, that you can't get in WH Smith). We could have the ability to choose – and pay for – what we wanted from that wide range.

The bad outcome is also simple to describe if I retain the print analogy. Our homes would be linked to two retailers. One would offer the products of the National Print Corporation, which we would all have by law to subscribe to, whether we wanted these products or not. The other would be a monopolistic and expensive version of WH Smith. A WH Smith that you can only enter if you have paid a substantial entrance fee, and where you can buy the *Daily Mail* provided you have also taken out a subscription to the *Radio Times*, the *Sunday Times*, *Cosmopolitan*, *Which?*, *Hello*, *Autocar*, and dozens of other publications, most of which you don't want and will never read. And, if you want a sports magazine, there will be a several available at a fancy price but all of them are WH Smith's own publications.

I am sure you recognise the television models behind my bad outcome: they are the BBC and Sky. To achieve the benefits of the revolution that is now under way, we have to do something serious about the BBC and Sky.

I think that, as citizens and consumers in a liberal democracy, we are generally best served if we can choose the products and services we want by paying for them directly. There are two major exceptions – health, and primary and secondary education, where, rightly in my view, most of the services are financed by taxation and are usually available free at the point of use, though those who can afford it can pay for alternatives.

Broadcasting is currently another exception. Until recently spectrum scarcity – that is, the extremely limited number of radio frequencies available for analogue broadcasting – fully justified this exemption from the workings of the free market. However, spectrum scarcity does not exist in the digital world, and we can have a free market in television if we want it.

My WH Smith analogy assumes we will be paying for our television. Free television – that is, television entirely funded by advertising – will still be available. But I think it will be more like an equivalent of print freesheets today than the wide-ranging and well-resourced services we currently get. And this is the subject of the next chapter.

3. The coming age of freesheet television

The problem with free television is that none of us pays for it directly. But how can this be a problem? Surely the existence of ITV for nearly 50 years, of Channel 4 for 20 years and of Channel 5 since 1997, financed entirely by advertising, has been of great value to British society?

Of course it has. And ITV and Channel 4 should be able – at least until the switch to digital – to perform something like their existing public service roles. However, both are facing pressures that affect the way they exercise these functions; each faces a different but serious strategic problem; and when analogue television is switched off both will lose most of the existing privileges that enable them to be commercially funded public service broadcasters. In the longer term I doubt therefore whether we can expect channels that rely purely on advertising to deliver the wide-ranging, diverse and well-resourced services we currently get.

In the first place there is the serious possibility that television's share of advertising in the UK is becoming less dynamic and losing something of its dominant position in the advertiser's world-view. One recent long-term advertising expenditure forecast suggested that television's share of advertising expenditure could drop from the 27.9 per cent it took in 2001 to 24.5 per cent in 2014.

Some leading figures in the industry are predicting a serious shift in advertiser behaviour away from television. There is a vigorous debate going on between those who proclaim that television's effectiveness as an advertising medium will continue for many years, and those who assert the increasing appeal of new media and alternative forms like direct mail. Whoever turns out to be right, the growth of new media is likely to have some effect on television's share; after all, newspapers and magazines had to adjust to the dramatic impact on their advertising revenues of the arrival of ITV 50 years ago.

A slowing growth in overall TV advertising revenues could be combined with a declining share of these revenues for the public service broadcasters as the competition from new channels increases. ITV's loss of share of audience and share of commercial revenue in recent years has been startling. Its share of audience has dropped from 33 per cent in 1997 to 24 per cent in 2003, and its share of TV advertising has also fallen dramatically (though falls in ITV advertising revenues are starting to plateau).

However, it is one of the ironies of the advertising market that, as audiences fragment, the advertisers are willing to pay even more for those channels with a mass reach, so the loss of audience share on ITV is not matched so far by a comparable loss of revenue.

While the future of TV advertising is unclear, the situation in the pay sectors is much more promising. Pay TV revenues, which are already approaching the £3.1 billion spent on TV advertising, are expected to continue to grow faster than TV advertising revenues.[9] The use of the TV screen for new purposes – games, DVDs, the internet – will continue to grow, and increasingly compete with the watching of conventional television programmes.

The income earned by these newcomers is beginning to rival that earned by ITV and Channel 4 – for example in 2003 the sales in the UK of computer games consoles and software came to over £2 billion, nearly as much as the advertising revenues of the two TV networks.[10] In the UK in 2002 we spent £1,056 million on buying and renting videos, and £1,451 million on buying and renting DVDs – significant increases on the previous year.[11]

Other changes will affect traditional broadcasters

At the same time there will be fundamental changes in the nature and purpose of other advertising-funded channels that will have an impact on the traditional broadcasters. I think that the overall outcome of all this will be that the range and quality of experiences available from free television will decline in comparison with the experiences that you can pay for. As more and more of us see this and act on this perception we will give another push to this cycle. Diversity, range and quality on free television are likely to become less and less available.

There is a truly perverse irony in the present situation. Nearly half the country has shown it is willing to pay more than £300 a year per household – on top of the £116 licence fee – to get extra TV channels and services, yet most of the services they get for that money are watched less – and, I would argue, are valued less – than the programmes they get for free. (Sky One, the most popular of the pure cable and satellite channels, had a 2.8 per cent share in multi-channel homes in 2003; the lowest share for a terrestrial channel in those homes was Channel 5's share of 6.3 per cent.) The unintended consequence of this is likely to be the undermining of programmes the multi-channel viewers really value, and of the British production base that provides, through secondary distribution, much of the programming they are paying to watch as repeats.

This is not sensible economics. Excluding sport and news, the great majority of original UK broadcast production comes from the BBC and the three commercial public service channels. You don't pay to watch the non-BBC programmes first time round – they come free. However, you do pay to watch repeats of these programmes on the cable and satellite services that are building businesses on showing old hits from the BBC, the ITV companies and Channel 4. Exactly the opposite happens with most imported US programmes, like *The Simpsons*. With these you pay to see them first; you only get to see them free a year or so later.

This must be the right way to do it, at least for high-value, high-cost programmes. You get the audience to pay for the privilege of seeing them first; those who don't want – or can't afford – to pay see them later on the free channels.

It is in my view hard to overestimate the significance of this perverse syndrome. We will pay more and more to watch and use television, yet we will not be paying to watch the programmes on ITV and Channel 4, however much we value them. Free television will decreasingly be able to provide the most expensive of these programmes. This either means there will be fewer such programmes – or producers and broadcasters will have to find a way of persuading audiences to pay for at least some of the programmes they presently get for free.

I recognise this will not be easy. We have seen from the short history of the internet how difficult it is for a medium that starts off being free to users to switch to one that is paid for. On the other hand Sky successfully overcame the hostility from viewers when the live football that people had watched for free on BBC and ITV was switched to Sky's pay channels. So it can be done.

Programmes that do not earn their keep

There is another long-standing feature of free television in Britain that is now becoming a serious structural problem. Some of the programmes that we enjoy most and respect most on ITV and Channel 4 do not earn their keep; at best they break even, at worst they are subsidised by other, more profitable genres.

By earn their keep I mean attract more in advertising revenue in the commercial breaks that surround them than it costs to make them. And this situation is getting worse. As the former managing director of Channel 4 International, Bernard Macleod, wrote in the *Financial Times*, 'the market is not working; the cost of certain types of programmes is not going down, and the price is not going up'.[12]

Macleod listed the kinds of programmes where the economics were in balance – 'soaps...quiz shows, talk shows, cookery shows, and others with a low cost base'. Children's shows could work because of 'the potential return from merchandising and publishing spin-offs'.

What wasn't working were 'large-scale drama, TV movies and high-end documentaries'. In other words the sort of programmes commercial public service broadcasters have traditionally been supposed to see as major public service obligations.

ITV and Channel 4 have always cross-subsidised loss-making or unprofitable productions from profitable ones. However, their ability to continue with this cross-subsidy is under pressure. More and more programmes are expected to pay their way. And, unlike some genres, expensive drama cannot easily exploit the new commercial opportunities being opened up by the new digital technologies.

Consider the great successes of ITV and Channel 4 in recent years – *Who Wants To Be A Millionaire*, *Pop Stars*, *Pop Idol*, *Big Brother*: so-called reality shows. The value of the *Pop Idol* or *Big Brother* type of programme to the broadcaster goes beyond the traditional commercial objectives – the high ratings and the sale of the format rights internationally. These programmes, with their multi-channel and multi-platform dimensions, with their new ways of engaging the audience (for example through voting), exploit the new digital technologies to generate important new revenues.

For instance, during *Big Brother* on Channel 4 in summer 2003 there were over 17 million votes and text messages from mobile phones and through the interactive facility on cable and satellite receivers, which brought in £4.3 million; and a further nearly £1 million was made from related games and quizzes. In total 4,339,805 voted in the 2003 *Big Brother* final, taking the total number of votes for the whole series to 11,993,636. In 2002 there were 8.6 million votes cast in the final and 22.7 million in the series.[13]

This money was split between the phone and platform operators, the channel and the programme producer. Understandably, this new link – between free television and new sources of commercial income – is beginning to affect the way broadcasters and producers decide what to make.

Of course someone has always had to pay for our free television. Thanks to a most elaborate regulatory framework, and to the peculiar historical anomaly of spectrum scarcity, we the audience have been able to avoid paying the usual price for being offered a free lunch. The adverts have been carefully corralled and strictly separated from the editorial content. If we wanted to, we have been able to ignore the fact that, basically, someone has been trying to get us to buy something.

This luxury is rapidly coming to an end. The basic nature of free television – that it is a promotional tool for commerce – is being exposed in an ever-increasing variety of ways. Programme sponsorship and advertising are still carefully regulated on the main terrestrial channels, though these rules are being periodically revised and relaxed as the financial pressures on the traditional broadcasters increase.

New ways to attract advertisers

Considerable ingenuity is used in finding new ways to secure the advertiser's support. We are now seeing serious attempts to get the advertiser directly involved in programme production. For example, a major British independent producer, the Television Corporation (maker of programmes like *Robot Wars*), has set up a special unit to develop advertiser-funded programmes. The creative initiative for these programmes comes from discussions between the producers and the advertiser, who is expected to provide up to half the cost of production. In return the advertiser is associated with all the non-broadcast exploitation of the programme. Once this agreement has been made, the programme idea is then sold to the television channel. One such series – *Britain's Worst Driver*, part-financed by E-Sure, the insurer – appeared on Channel 5 in autumn 2002 and again in 2003.

Several years ago new rules were introduced to allow shopping channels (like QVC) on to cable and satellite. Now the man who thought up FreeServe for Dixons is trying to interest retailers and financial services in creating their own individual channels. Peter Wilkinson, the main shareholder in the Digital Interactive Television Group, told the *Guardian* in September 2002 that 'brands' could launch a television channel for as little as £1 million a year – 'not even a pin-prick in their annual marketing budgets' – and use these to persuade viewers to buy goods through the remote controls.[14]

That is a direct and unabashed use of the medium for retail

purposes. However, a subtler and more wide-ranging commercial approach is becoming available for traditional broadcasters, even with their diverse schedules of conventional programmes.

One of the candidates interviewed for the Channel 4 chief executive job in the autumn of 2001 advocated that we should adopt the 'Martha Stewart' strategy. Martha Stewart is now famous for getting caught up in the wave of Wall Street financial scandals, but at that time she was well known purely as one of the great American media icons – a woman who had built a commercial empire in the US on cookery and lifestyle products. The key feature of her strategy that Channel 4 was being encouraged to adopt was that her TV programmes played a critical part in an integrated process of getting people to buy a wide range of goods and services available under the Martha Stewart brand. Free television was the vital promotional tool, but the real money was made elsewhere. Channel 4, this candidate argued, was well placed to design a raft of programmes on this basis and take a large part of the revenues these would generate.

The candidate didn't get the job, but in one way his logic was compelling. Indeed it is being followed by a terrestrial European TV channel that offers an interesting model for the future – M6 in France. M6 has in 15 years turned itself into the second largest commercial broadcaster in France. It has a strong appeal to the 16–34 age group, and uses a significant number of its programmes to promote and support its own record label, its cinema and DVD distribution, its magazines, its merchandising, its home shopping and its events. Over half of its revenues comes from these activities; in effect the free TV channel is a shop window for the new businesses it is steadily creating or acquiring. And, while the free TV channel is growing very slowly, the new businesses are growing very rapidly. Understandably, the programme schedule is influenced by this underlying business strategy.

Because of their regulatory restrictions and obligations, neither ITV nor Channel 4 could pursue such strategies – at least in their full-blooded versions – at the moment. Nonetheless a more modest and piecemeal version is, in my view, likely to be taken up by both services in future, since they will need to compensate as best they can for any decline in their shares of TV advertising revenues.

The essential reality of free television is coming to the surface. And unsurprisingly some viewers are beginning to react to it. An OFTEL survey in the summer of 2001 found that most pay TV viewers now assumed that quality television meant subscription television.

Summary

To summarise the problems facing our mainstream free broadcasters:

○ Television advertising – their bedrock income – is very unlikely to grow at the rate it has done for the past 20 years, and its share of overall advertising expenditure could decline.

○ ITV's share of TV audiences and advertising has been falling steadily for several years, though Channel 4's share of both has until this year been stable; the pressure on both networks to maximise revenues from each programme will intensify.

○ Costs of both original production and acquired material are rising, and important programme genres that they are required to broadcast cannot earn their keep.

○ The new revenue opportunities opening up in the multi-channel and digital world will tempt broadcasters to regard their programme schedules as both a direct and indirect way of getting viewers to spend money on products and services in which the broadcaster has a direct commercial stake.

Avoiding the problems created by this structural threat to the business models on which commercial public service broadcasting had previously relied, while enhancing the range of choice and quality offered to the public, would require a strategy that enabled all the major current broadcasters to reinvent themselves for a digital environment. These changes would have to occur simultaneously, through a mix of political decision-making and vision, regulatory adaptation, and organisational strategy by the broadcasters themselves.

The next chapters address the specific challenges and opportunities facing each of the major current players: ITV, Sky, Channel 4 and the BBC.

4. ITV – a lesson in decline?

The gloomy ITV story of recent years can be characterised in various ways. One of the easiest is to blame it on poor management. No doubt there is some truth in this, but I think the real story has a more fundamental feature. There was a failure of public policy to understand in good time the scale of the technological and industrial revolution that was being unleashed with the end of spectrum scarcity, and a failure to understand the implications of that revolution for ITV in particular. Because of our attachment to past glories, we have allowed a major national asset to waste away steadily.

I remember feeling, when I was director of the ITV Association in the mid-1990s, how much policy-makers seemed to take ITV for granted. It was very difficult to get them to give serious consideration to the possibility that the peculiar structural features of ITV were going to threaten the network's ability to fulfil the functions laid down for it. Regrettably, it probably is a basic condition of a politically enabled and regulated industry like public service broadcasting that democratic politicians will never feel able to deal with a problem until it is so severe that pretty well everyone accepts that there is one. Only when it is seriously and visibly broke will anyone get round to fixing it.

The heart of the problem has been the Broadcasting Act 1990. In many ways this was a radical piece of legislation (though not as radical as the 1988 white paper that preceded it). It saw that a federation of 15 companies, none of them big in business terms, would need to be allowed to consolidate. However, the Act set up such a limited process of consolidation that it needed to be changed six years later – and was changed again another six years after that. Reform was eked out rather than embraced. At the same time the Act created a competition regime that set in stone a structure for the core of ITV's business – the commissioning and scheduling of the network programmes – which might have worked well for ITV had it been in place in the 1980s but turned out to be a serious handicap in the 1990s. The new system made it very difficult for the major ITV companies to tie their programme-making decisions to the commercial consequences of those decisions.

Basically, the ITV companies had to compete with each other and with the independent producers to provide programmes to the network centre – newly created by the 1990 Act as an independent body, even though it was entirely funded by the companies. (The tendering system set up by the Act also created fierce internal divisions over the network budget, since companies that had bid high for their licences had less to spend on programmes than those that had bid low.)

Previously the major companies had had a guaranteed place in the network schedule for their programmes, and while there were serious flaws in this system it at least maintained a partial link between what the individual companies produced and the income they earned from the airtime sold around the programmes. The 1990 Act completely broke this link, just at the moment – with the arrival of competition for advertising revenue from Channel 4, Sky and (a bit later) Channel 5 – when ITV needed a more focused and integrated programme strategy, not a more diffused one.

It is difficult to overstate the adverse consequences of this new system. The energies of the ITV companies were largely directed inwards. These were spent working out how to take each other over, or, if you expected to be a target, how to secure the best price for surrender: in fighting each other for commissions from the network; in pressuring the network director to commission your projects and pressuring him again to put the best programmes in the slots that suited your sales house rather than someone else's; and in fighting your own news organisation, as well as the government and the regulator, over where its bulletins should go. None of ITV's rivals – the BBC, Channels 4 and 5, Sky – had these difficulties. Their energies could be and generally were directed outwards, against the competition (though sometimes the BBC did manage to look as if it too was more interested in fighting its own internal battles).

It is of course easy to see why this happened. The regional structure of ITV has been for most of its existence one of its great glories. For the 30 years of an almost total advertising monopoly we could afford to see a dozen well-resourced company headquarters and production centres dispersed around the country, from Aberdeen to Plymouth. These were a source of pride (and employment) to the people of the regions, and – perhaps more importantly – to the region's MPs, many of whom could expect regular exposure on peak-time local programmes. The major production centres outside London – particularly in Manchester and Leeds – produced network programmes as good as those made by the London companies; and these were often programmes rooted in the culture of the regions they came from. (*Coronation Street* and *Emmerdale* are ongoing examples of this.) It was for many years a very good system, and it is understandable that many people have resisted any attempt by the companies to weaken their regional obligations. Economic pressures have inevitably undermined this system.

We do not, however, need to abolish the ITV regional licensing structure. There is real ongoing value in allowing separate companies in Ulster, Scotland and the Channel Islands, even though there is now one big English company. And it will be right to expect this English company to provide good-quality local news services in the regions and sub-regions that currently have them, and for several years yet – certainly until digital switchover – to be obliged to make network productions in centres outside London.

ITV in the digital world

The new legislation that has permitted the recent merger of Carlton and Granada also permits this English ITV to be American-owned, a provision that has provoked considerable controversy. My own view is that this revision to the ownership rules will be neither as catastrophic as its critics suggest nor as risk-free as the government seems to think. (It is certainly not as dangerous as the repeal of the cross-media rules restricting the newspaper ownership of Channel 5, a reform that would allow Sky and Channel 5 to merge.) As with many – perhaps too many – of the Act's provisions, the actual outcome will depend on the effectiveness of the new regulator, Ofcom. In this case it needs to ensure that whoever owns ITV continues to invest heavily in large-scale original British production.

However, these changes are not enough to ensure that ITV in the digital world will still be able to do the job it currently does. The really profound reform would be to allow the ITV companies to charge viewers to watch some of their programmes if they wanted to – and this is still not permitted in the Communications Act.

However, the Act probably does allow ITV to find a more effective kind of relationship between its free service and other commercial activities. There is a risk that this will result in due course in ITV joining the ranks of what I have called freesheet television, that is, television that is almost entirely determined by the needs of the advertisers. How much this matters rather depends on what happens elsewhere – to the BBC, Channel 4, and in pay television. (Freesheets, incidentally, are fine, provided they are not all we have. The London give-away newspaper *Metro* is succinct and crisply written, but you don't expect to find there the same range and quality of journalism that you get in a broadsheet.)

ITV is a profitable network. We can reasonably expect it to provide some kind of public service broadcasting in return for its privileged position, at least until we switch from analogue to digital broadcasting. I believe it would be wise for both Ofcom and Parliament to recognise that a quality news service, a high level of original production, and a more limited regional service, are the most we can expect from ITV in this respect – the rest will have to be left to their commercial skills and judgements.

But we also need to recognise that the economic context in which free television operates is changing fast, and with it the expectations we can and should have of it. In few other areas of economic activity do we expect something that is provided free to have the same quality as something for which we pay – whether the payment is through taxation or the marketplace.

5. Paying the piper but not calling the tune

Earlier I argued that the combination of various new technologies – in particular broadband delivery systems, personal video recorders with substantial memories and sophisticated intelligence, and micro-payment systems – could enable most of us to shop for our television programmes and products from home in much the same way as we now shop for books, magazines and newspapers from retailers like WH Smith, Waterstone's and the corner newsagent. We could pay for individual programmes, and subscribe to individual channels or combinations of them. There will be a number of purely advertiser-funded services, but many of these are likely to be much more obviously tools for the promotion of commercial products and services than they are now.

In such a world the role of public service broadcasting will be radically transformed. As I will argue in detail in the next chapter, we should lose the licence fee for television (though probably not for radio), so that after digital switchover the BBC would become largely funded by subscriptions, and eventually – if it so wished – by advertising as well; and ITV and Channel 4 should also be allowed to charge for their programmes if they wish to. In this way producers would get the maximum value from their programmes, and most viewers and consumers could choose freely from a wide range of offerings.

However, this outcome could well be thwarted by two major

institutions – the BBC and Sky. In this chapter I look at the problems posed by the way digital television is developing in Britain, and in particular the challenge presented by the dominance of Sky in pay television.

If the problem with free television is that none of us pays for it, and if the problem with the BBC is that we all have to pay for it whether or not we want it, then the problem with digital television is that we cannot just pay for what we want.

Let me remind you of the analogy I used earlier. If we cannot change the structure of the pay TV market in crucial ways, the future version of an electronic WH Smith will be very unfriendly to consumers. We will pay to go into the shop, and only be able to buy a newspaper if we buy two or three others as well, plus a raft of magazines and books. In addition we will find that some of the most popular products are made exclusively by the shop owner, who uses this monopoly to discourage you from trying other shops – not that there will be many of these available – while being able to charge you whatever he wants for his exclusive offerings.

We would not tolerate such a situation in the press and book publishing markets. So we need to understand why we seem to be tolerating its development in digital television, and find ways of preventing it reaching this unattractive conclusion.

How we got here

First, a brief account of the advantages of digital over analogue television. As a transmission mechanism, digital is substantially more efficient: it uses less power, and it can deliver many more services. It delivers a better widescreen picture. A digital receiver is a much more sophisticated machine than an analogue one: it can store and manipulate material on a significant scale and, if it is connected to a telecoms network, enable instant transactions. In the digital world, the traditional television set will effectively be transformed into a screen linked to a computer.

Given these advantages and opportunities it is not very surprising that around ten years ago broadcasters, equipment manufacturers and governments in the US, Europe and Japan became enthusiastic about the potential of the new digital technologies. Broadcasters saw the chance to transmit many more services cheaply and the opportunity to develop very different kinds of services. Manufacturers saw the chance of reviving a flagging sector of the consumer electronics market. Governments saw all these advantages, plus the chance to exploit one of their national assets – the radio spectrum – in radical new ways, most of which might generate substantial public revenues.

However, the introduction of digital television would need not only billions of pounds of investment, but a novel kind of cooperation between governments, broadcasters and manufacturers, some of it on an international scale. The radio spectrum would need to be reallocated, a lot of it by international agreement. There would have to be new technical standards, ideally agreed by all those involved – but these agreements would have to embrace the telecoms and information technology sectors as well as the broadcasters.

Persuading viewers and consumers to join the digital revolution would be even more problematic. It was obvious that digital and analogue systems would have to run in parallel, sometimes for many years, which would be both wasteful and expensive, particularly for the broadcasters.

Unfortunately we have only partly achieved a rational, cooperative policy in Europe. Rival broadcasters refused to agree a comprehensive set of standards for the new technologies – owning a proprietary standard, or having exclusive use of it in a particular territory, could enable you to get an armlock on a particular pay TV market.

Neither Brussels nor the national governments were prepared to prevent the development of what were de facto pay TV monopolies. In part this was a reaction to an earlier unsuccessful attempt by the European Commission to impose a high-definition TV standard on broadcasters in the late 1980s and early 1990s – the Commission decided to leave such matters largely to the industry in future. In part it was a belief in government that only by allowing big companies to reap the rewards of a monopoly would they be prepared to invest the large sums needed for the introduction of the new technologies.

A 1977 international agreement allocating satellite broadcasting frequencies to each country allowed Britain to introduce pay TV in the late 1980s for the first time.[15] In France around the same time a terrestrial pay TV channel was started – Canal Plus. Both countries intended these to be regulated national monopolies in the first instance. Canal Plus successfully played this role in France, but the plan didn't work in Britain; the consortium that won the satellite licence here was BSB. Unfortunately for BSB Rupert Murdoch, who had been prevented by the Independent Broadcasting Authority (IBA) from running an ITV company in the early 1970s, decided to bypass the UK government and the regulator by hiring space on the Luxemburg satellite, Astra, even though this used frequencies designed for telecommunications rather than broadcasting. In 1989 Murdoch launched the Sky pay TV services in competition with the fledgling BSB.

This competition – almost unique in the new satellite pay TV markets starting around the world – nearly bled both companies to death. Late in 1990 they were forced to agree a merger, though it was Murdoch who became the dominant shareholder, and it was his management that ran the new BSkyB. Just as important, the new company used the Astra satellite and the Murdoch pay technology. Thus, unlike what was happening in France, Britain's pay TV champion would be foreign-owned and largely outside the national regulatory regime.

As a result UK governments and regulators have been able to dodge many of the hard decisions about competition in digital television, and our expanding pay TV market continues to be dominated by a single vertically integrated operator – that is, one that owns or controls both the production and distribution businesses. It has also meant that there are a number of competing digital technologies now well established in people's homes, some of which are incompatible with each other. As a result we have neither the benefits of monopoly – a single technology standard – nor the benefits of robust competition between a sufficient number of rival commercial operators.

This represents a serious failure of public policy on an issue of great commercial and cultural importance, which has occurred because successive UK governments have been unwilling to act effectively. It is possible that the new regulatory regime created by the Communications Act will over time be able to remedy this. If so, the new people at Ofcom will have to do better than their predecessors in Oftel and the Office of Fair Trading (OFT), whose decisions in this area have so far had only a modest impact on the pay TV market, and whose overall record has been unsatisfactory.

Consider the most recent example. The result of a three-year OFT inquiry into the prices Sky charged its rivals for its premium sports and film channels was announced on 17 December 2002, to considerable surprise. Despite its preliminary finding a year earlier that it expected to find Sky guilty, the OFT eventually decided that there were 'insufficient grounds' for concluding it had broken the law. Sky was deemed to be on the 'border' of anti-competitive behaviour, said the OFT. Perhaps that was meant as a warning to Sky to moderate its practices – though that was not how its frustrated rivals seemed to take it. (Those that were still around, that is – one of the original complainants, ITV Digital, had died in the meantime.)

It is important to understand why we cannot as viewers and consumers just pay to get the channels we want; and why the current market structures may well prevent the emergence of a true, consumer-friendly market for many years – even though the technologies exist that would enable such a market.

Strategic moves by Sky in the early 1990s

Sky made three very smart strategic moves when it started its pay service in the early 1990s. First, it was able to control the key technology needed for satellite pay TV services in the UK through its sister News Corporation company, News Datacom (now NDS), which had developed its own encryption system. Second, it bought exclusive rights to films and sport, the most attractive pay TV services. It then used these two powerful technology and rights assets to create a comprehensive retail package for satellite viewers, which effectively eliminated the possible emergence of any satellite competitor.

Sky was able to ensure that almost every pay TV channel had to join the Sky satellite package on its terms. When satellite television first started, nearly all channels were financed by advertising, and people bought dishes from different manufacturers. When Sky set up a subscription service it provided the dishes itself and ensured these could effectively receive only services that were encrypted using the News Datacom technology. This gave it the whip hand over any channel wanting to generate subscription revenues – which, given the losses they were sustaining, soon came to mean nearly all of them. Even the powerful American operators like MTV and Disney had to join the new regime on Sky's terms eventually.

At the same time Sky made sure that rival cable (and, later, terrestrial) pay operators could only get the Sky premium sport and film channels on highly disadvantageous terms. (And these were of course the services that prompted most people to think about getting pay TV.) Though Sky created this business model in the analogue world of the early 1990s, the operator has successfully migrated it to what ought to have been the far more competitive digital world of today.

An imperfect market

The result has been that there has been no effective competition either within the UK satellite market, or between different pay TV operators, particularly in the provision of alternative film and sports channels. Sky has undoubtedly been better organised and better managed than its rivals, but it has also been extremely ruthless in its behaviour. Indeed, given that the cable companies have to offer their viewers the Sky film and sport channels more expensively than Sky does, the only reason that they have been able to compete at all is because they have been able to combine TV and telephone services in retail packages that do have some real value to potential customers.

The two big ITV companies, Carlton and Granada, did eventually try to challenge Sky's domination of pay TV sport, by creating a rival channel – ITV Sport – based on their exclusive rights to the European Champions league and the Nationwide football league in the UK. However, they were unable to agree terms with either Sky or Telewest, the second cable company, to carry this new service, though they did reach agreement with ntl. This inevitably meant that the financial calculations on which they had acquired these rights were completely undermined. ITV's subsequent failure to persuade the Nationwide league football clubs to renegotiate the terms of their agreement in March 2002 did not just lead to the collapse of the ITV Sport channel but was an important factor in the collapse of ITV Digital, the terrestrial pay TV platform, as well.

So instead of competition between three digital platforms – satellite, cable and terrestrial – as the government had intended, we now have only two pay TV contenders. And, with the enormous debt burdens ntl and Telewest have incurred, the cable companies are not – at the moment at least – providing much competition to Sky either.

Sky's dominance

Why exactly is Sky's dominance a problem? After all, Sky's services are clearly popular – over seven million people subscribe to them,[16] and a good number of these could have chosen a cable competitor if they had wanted to. No one is obliged to watch pay TV; indeed nearly half the country, after a decade of expensive marketing from pay TV operators, has chosen to do without it, and the current evidence is that a significant number say that they will never want it.

There are two serious difficulties with this. The first is that it is disingenuous to suppose that we do not need to worry about the position of the seven million Sky subscribers. They have to swallow whatever price increases Sky imposes – if they don't like them they have nowhere else to go to get the services at a lower price. Sky has seen off one competitor – ITV Digital – and can prevent its cable rivals from offering lower prices than it does. It is surely a highly unsatisfactory situation for consumers where the only choice is to like it or lump it.

Second, why do Sky (or indeed cable) viewers have to accept a situation where they cannot buy whatever mix of channels and services they want? Three-quarters of Sky subscribers pay for a premium package – one that includes either films or sports. Yet, even though it is to get these services that they sign up for pay TV in the first place, they cannot buy the films or sports channels on their own. The reason is straightforward. Sky does not make much of its profits from these premium services; it makes them from all the other channels in the basic tier, which all pay viewers have to subscribe to in one form or another. If people could choose simply to buy the sport or film services, Sky's business would have to be seriously restructured.

This is well known to the competition authorities, who are supposed to look after the interests of the consumers in these matters. So why have they accepted this situation? There have been two main reasons: they believe, first, that Sky is entitled to recover the £2 billion it has invested in moving to digital over the past six years; and, second, that the consumer has benefited from the practice of bundling channels, and from requiring those who want to watch premium channels to pay for the basic tier first. The argument is that without such compulsion many of these channels could not have established themselves. In this way consumer choice has overall been enhanced by the great increase in the number of TV channels available, even if individuals are paying for scores of channels they never watch and would never dream of watching.

These are reasonable propositions, but implicit in them is that there must come a time when neither any longer applies. Sky will soon have paid off its debts and is now starting to make handsome profits. (In 2003 BSkyB returned its first annual pre-tax profit in five years. The company reported that it had returned a core pre-tax profit of £260 million in the year to 30 June while turnover had grown 15 per cent to £3.19 billion. In 2002 the company made a loss of £22 million.)[17]

At some point the hundreds of pay channels currently retailed by Sky should be expected to stand or fall on their intrinsic appeal to consumers. It is, as I once suggested to members of the Competition

Commission in a DTI seminar, a bit like going into a supermarket to buy a chicken, and being told you could only have the chicken if you bought soap powder, fruit juice, an assortment of pickles, frozen pizza, a bottle of shampoo, a packet of bin liners and a block of ice cream as well. They said they hadn't thought of it like that, which didn't seem much of an answer. We will now have to wait to see how soon Ofcom chooses to get involved in these matters.

The issue of unbundling channels and enabling true consumer choice is the more important because in the all-digital future the majority of us are likely to get our TV programmes from Sky, ntl and Telewest, and BT's broadband network rather than via terrestrial networks, though these could be the main providers to the second and third sets in people's homes. The good news is that BT is already trying to create a broadband market where people can make small transactions, costing only a few pounds or even pence – a micro-payment system.[18] (Such systems are now well established in Germany, and are increasingly popular.) Sky's most advanced receiver – Sky-Plus, which includes a powerful personal video recorder – has a slot which could be used for such payments, though the company has not yet found a viable business model for this kind of transaction.

Not that there is much pressure on Sky to adapt its current highly successful business model. One aspect of Sky's treatment of its suppliers that causes particular frustration is that the latter have no idea who is paying to receive their services. The list of subscribers is owned by Sky and is not made available to any of the pay channels that it retails. Thus Channel 4 does not know which satellite viewers take Film Four, for example – unlike print magazines and journals, which have a direct relationship with all their subscribers and take care to nurture them. Sky's behaviour also contrasts with that of British Telecom, which lets the businesses that use its broadband services know who their customers are.

Sky's relationship with its supplier channels

One final example of what I regard as a regressive trend in satellite pay TV: as Sky starts to renegotiate the terms on which it pays subscriber fees to its supplier channels, it is in general reducing them substantially (it is not, of course, passing these reductions on to its subscribers). It can do this because pay TV channels depend on Sky for their existence, and have little bargaining power. This in turn makes them more reliant on advertising income. I believe we need to be moving in the opposite direction, towards a world where most channels and programmes are at least in part paid for directly by the consumer. Only in this way can we develop a conventional market where people can freely choose what they want to spend their money on. Sky's interest is indeed to get people to pay more – but more to Sky, not anyone else.

This feature of the pay TV market – that the platform operator determines the price paid by the subscriber for a channel as well as the price the operator will pay to the channel – needs to be reformed if we are to enable the producers of programmes and the channel providers to deliver better quality television in the digital era.

Newspapers and magazines determine the price at which their products are sold in the shops. The situation is different in book publishing, where the abolition of the net book agreement a few years ago has meant that booksellers can discount the price at which some books are sold. But the booksellers can't drive the price they pay the publishers down too far – there is sufficient competition between them to give the publishers some protection.

Similarly in telecoms: suppliers to the new broadband micro-payment market that BT set up last year choose the price they wish to charge for their products. BT charges them a service fee on a sliding scale based on volume of traffic.

It is vital that pay TV operators are required by the regulators to move in this direction – otherwise there is far too little reward for quality. The current structure – of a vast number of so-called basic channels and a handful of premium ones – is crude: consumers cannot express much of a preference between the different channels, nor express that preference through a willingness to pay more for those they want most.

From Sky's point of view, this is an excellent situation, and if you were Sky you would have little wish to change it. And that is why I doubt whether we will be able to move to the kind of market I described at the beginning of this chapter – where you can buy what television you like in a way that most suits you – without much more serious legislative or regulatory intervention than we have seen hitherto.

What can be done?

So what needs to be done? The first thing is that Ofcom should as soon as possible revisit – and hopefully reform – the unbundling and buy-through practices that the ITC left in place when it renewed these in 1998. Sky is now profitable – it no longer needs the economic prop of forcing viewers into the basic and premium packages that it has operated for more than ten years.

It is likely that, if present practice were changed in this way, some of the current channels with very low viewing figures would not survive. So what? The multi-channel world is securely established. By all means let a thousand channels bloom, but let them survive on their ability to win customers and audiences.

The second reform is tighter regulation of the pricing structures of pay TV, so that the platform operators – Sky and the cable companies – cannot solely determine the price at which channels – and in due course, individual programmes – are sold. The existence of this feature is of particular concern in the television market. Here there are only a couple of retailers; the suppliers are in a particularly weak bargaining position, and the operator can force the supplier to rely on an alternative source of funding through selling advertising. For democratic and cultural reasons we need to ensure diversity and quality of supply: leaving this to the commercial judgements of a handful of platform operators is unlikely to be enough to guarantee these crucial outcomes.

The third possible reform is for Ofcom in due course to consider whether to require Sky to separate carriage – its business as a platform operator – from content – its business as a channel provider – Sky Sports, Sky One, and so on. This move was advocated by the

BBC, Channel 4 and the *Guardian* in the run-up to the Communications Bill. Such a separation would turn the Sky satellite platform into something more like a common carrier, with no opportunity for bias towards its own channels and against others designed to compete with them for audiences and revenue.

This would be a drastic move; and perhaps the mere prospect of it would persuade Sky to abandon today's world of channel bundling and buy-through to premium channels. But, then again, perhaps it wouldn't. I do not envy Lord Currie and his new Ofcom board the difficulties they will face if they decide to enable the viewers of digital television to pay only for the channels they want to watch, not dozens and dozens that they don't. Nonetheless, we have to hope they have the stomach for the task.

6. The reformation of the BBC

The problem with the BBC is that we have to pay for it, whether we want it or not. Developments in technology offer us the chance over the next ten years of moving away from the very peculiar industry structure we currently have in broadcasting towards a much more conventional model, where we buy and use TV products in much the way we now buy and use print. Instead of getting most of our television free at the point of use, we would have a variety of choices, many of them involving paying for what we watched.

This shift to a conventional market is, on balance, a desirable development. However, the BBC has as great an interest as BSkyB in preventing this from happening. Very obviously, a situation where people can essentially choose what TV they pay for implies the end of the poll tax we call the licence fee, and with it a fundamental reformation of the BBC.

This has of course been an issue for many years. Back in 1985, the Peacock Committee was set up by the Thatcher government to look at alternatives to the licence fee. The Committee rejected the idea of funding the BBC by advertising (since this would force it into direct competition with ITV, with what were then deemed to be unacceptable consequences), but argued, presciently, that the technological changes then in their infancy would put an end to spectrum scarcity. When this happened, Peacock said, the BBC should rely to a great extent on voluntary subscription.[19]

That hasn't yet happened. The full consequences of technological change have been slower to emerge than Peacock anticipated. Even more important, the BBC has significantly improved its performance since the mid-1980s – in efficiency and value for money in particular. The BBC has been able to rely on both a degree of positive public support and the absence of any significant popular demand for change to keep suggestions for radical reformation off the political agenda – at least until very recently.

In 1999 the question of the licence fee was again addressed in another major report, this time by the Davies Committee, set up to consider if and how the BBC should fund additional digital services. It came out for an increase in the fee – but it also offered a significant caveat for the future of the fee. Davies conceded in his report that it was 'quite conceivable that the world would develop in the direction envisaged by Peacock' and '[would bring] broadcasting tolerably close to a perfect market….If the broadcasting market were ever to approach the condition of the book publishing market, it would be much more dubious whether the BBC and the licence fee could be justified in their present role'.[20]

Four years on from the Davies report it is now much more obvious that that 'near-perfect market' is attainable – if we have the political will to make it happen. The combination of broadband delivery, personal video recorders and micro-billing payment systems could enable us to buy TV programmes much as we buy books and newspapers. But to achieve this we have to get rid of the roadblock that is the BBC in its current form. Earlier I likened the BBC to a National Print Corporation, funded by a poll tax, swamping the publishing market with its subsidised output. I doubt that even socialists would today argue for such an entity in print.

Arguments for and against a continued licence fee

What are the arguments used in defence of a continued licence fee? The first is that broadcasting is what economists call a 'public good'. Once a TV programme has been produced, the cost of an additional viewer is zero. If people had to pay to watch individual programmes, this would restrict viewing to those who choose to pay the fee and would exclude those who might watch it if it were free. This would be a loss to society overall.

Broadcasting is also a 'merit good' – something whose value exceeds the estimation an individual might place on it. (Other examples quoted in Davies are museums and galleries.) 'If', said Davies, 'all television is provided by the free market, there is a danger that consumers will under-invest in the development of their own tastes, experience and capacity to comprehend.'[21]

Other factors adduced by Davies in favour of a public institution like the BBC were the likely concentration of ownership, thanks to the economies of scale that operate in broadcasting, replacing one sort of monopoly – spectrum scarcity – with another, commercially created monopoly. At the same time the increase in channels would lead to audience fragmentation, which, since the cost of production would remain high, would increase average costs. In short, market failure was likely to occur even in the future imagined by Peacock, requiring public intervention to correct this.

My difficulty is that I can accept much of this description of the potential for market failure without concluding with Davies that the BBC is the answer to the problem. We do not, for example, deal with the 'merit good' issue as it affects museums and galleries by creating a British Gallery Corporation to own and run nearly half the country's museums. We rightly value the diversity we get from a large number of independent institutions. And I would question quite how much of the current BBC1 output truly justifies inclusion under the 'merit good' heading.

Why not retain the BBC in its current form?

Still, the BBC exists in the form it does, however anachronistic that may seem to people like me. It is successful. In an uncertain future, which might see ITV owned by one American global giant and our pay TV industry dominated by Sky, why not hang on to the one institution on which we can rely to produce high-quality original British programming?

One answer is for the new regulator, Ofcom, to exercise its powers to prevent our commercial electronic media being dominated by, for example, Disney and News Corporation. Having the BBC as a public service monopolist doesn't seem much of a democratic solution – after all, it was because of the concern about the monopoly power of the BBC in the new world of television in the 1950s that Parliament created the ITV network. The fact that ITV might no longer be a sufficient counterweight means we need to look for other solutions, not revert to depending on the BBC alone to achieve the social and cultural objectives that we have traditionally included in our broadcasting policy.

Anyway, these objectives need re-examination. Should it, for example, be important for television to act as a unifying force for the country, bringing us all together in a great community of viewers sharing a common experience? Greg Dyke – the BBC's director-general until he was forced to resign following the publication of the Hutton report in January 2004 – recently repeated the view that this is one of the fundamental purposes of the BBC.[22]

That the BBC and ITV – though more usually the BBC – have regularly provided this kind of 'social glue' for nearly 50 years is an accident of engineering and history. The engineering has changed – we no longer depend on the limited terrestrial broadcast frequencies to deliver our television – and we can therefore change our future history.

I would argue that it is not the sign of a mature democracy to have very much of this 'voice of the nation' stuff, and certainly not healthy to either expect or allow one institution to regard itself as The Voice of the Nation when it comes to major national occasions.

We certainly wouldn't expect to find such an institution among our newspapers – I suppose *The Times* once fancied itself in this role, at least for the governing classes, but thankfully it lost it long ago. Now is the time to get the BBC to drop it, too. After all it was the BBC itself that produced, several years ago, an analysis of contemporary Britain that divided us into a hundred tribes, reflecting the fact that our tastes, backgrounds and aspirations diverge greatly. Characteristically the BBC concluded from its research that it was its job to serve all these hundred tribes, since they all paid the licence fee. Another conclusion – and one with rather more logic – would be to recognise that the hundred tribes might be better served if their TV viewing came from a wide number of organisations, many designed to cater for specific tastes. And if this undermines the concept of the licence fee, so be it.

However, I recognise that there is one social and cultural objective that is likely to retain its legitimacy even in a Peacock-style perfect market. That is to provide everyone, however poor they might be, with access to news and information of a reasonable quality. But this objective can be achieved in a number of different ways. If we want to live in a diverse and pluralist world, then preserving an institution like the BBC as the primary – or even only – way to deliver this objective is a very poor way of solving the access problem.

I have two main reasons for saying this. The first derives from the kind of institution that the BBC is. It is in effect a self-perpetuating department of state but without an elected politician at the head of it. Like other departments of state it is funded by tax-payers' money, but unlike them it is guaranteed more money than it needs to do the job for which it has been created. Indeed it is more powerful than most department of states – certainly more powerful than the Department of Culture, Media and Sport that is supposed to hold it to account, despite the brave efforts of Tessa Jowell to operate her supervisory role in a principled way. And, unlike his power over other departments of state, the Prime Minister can't simply break it up, reshuffle it, merge it with another department or replace the people running it.

By this I don't mean that the BBC is part of the government – far from it. It is worse than that. We can at least get rid of the government at a general election. We have no effective way of registering dissatisfaction with the BBC as an institution – we can't stop paying for it, which is our normal recourse with services we have a quarrel with. Of course if most of us stopped watching its programmes this would have a big effect; but this is precisely what the BBC understandably bends all its efforts to prevent – and given its extraordinarily privileged position, it would take extraordinary incompetence to lose viewers on such a scale.

In short the BBC is, in its current form, a cultural tyranny – a largely benevolent one, admittedly, but a tyranny nonetheless. I think historians a hundred years from now will wonder how a liberal democratic country tolerated such an institution for so long.

I recognise that many people will balk at this description of an admired organisation. (Indeed the veteran Tory journalist Peregrine Worsthorne described the BBC as the only great institution created in Britain in the twentieth century.)[23] But even fans of the BBC ought to be concerned at the developments that furnish me with my second reason for arguing that the time has come to reform it radically. The BBC is regularly criticised for being too commercial, particularly in respect of BBC1. There is indeed some justice in this criticism, though I personally have sympathy for the BBC's attempts to redefine the roles of its various TV channels. It is a valid way of dealing with the changes that are happening in society and broadcasting. Anyway the tension between being popular and being high-minded is endemic in all forms of public service broadcasting, and is an increasing dilemma for ITV and Channel 4 as well as the BBC.

Today's broadcasting is about winning

The fundamental problem is that the centre of gravity in Britain's programme-making community has shifted significantly. The definition of personal success in television is now as much financial as creative. The heroes of today's programme-making culture are admired for making money as well as making programmes. (The trade magazine *Broadcast* now produces an annual 'Rich list of the 100 wealthiest people in TV broadcasting and production'.) One of the most powerful role models is the independent producer who builds a company to the point where it can be sold for millions of pounds to a broadcaster or major international media company, or whose formats are bought by the big American networks. This is a relatively new model and one with a truly subversive character.

As someone who benefited handsomely from an LWT share option scheme in the early 1990s, I am in no position to deplore this development: and indeed I don't think there is anything wrong with creative success being rewarded in this way. However, we do need to recognise what the new business ethos in programme-making is doing to the culture itself. When I started in television more than 30 years ago no one came into programme-making to make money; you could have a very comfortable life but only the stars, not the producers or directors, could hope to end up as millionaires.

You came in because it was fun, exciting – and in many cases because you thought you could improve the world through making documentaries, or current affairs programmes, or serious drama. Producing TV programmes was, for many people, about making society better, not about making a fortune.

That was, self-evidently, a culture and ethos well suited to a broadcasting system dedicated to public service ideals. An ethos that esteems those who enrich themselves through their creativity is not. And that is the real problem – for the BBC as well as for the rest of us. Public service broadcasting is being hollowed out from within. The ambitious programme-makers of today cannot really afford to subscribe to such old-fashioned ideals, even if they want to – and I am not sure how many of them want to. One journalist who left the BBC current affairs department recently described how he and his colleagues felt like 'second-class citizens' in a BBC where the admired factual programmes are those that fulfilled an entertainment function, not a journalistic one.

Of course there are many older producers who still carry a public service torch, even if the demand for their programmes and their ideas is diminishing by the year. And I hope there are some young researchers and producers who still want to make the world a better place through their programmes – if the opportunity to do so should ever occur. And sometimes, on BBC2 and BBC4, on Channel 4, the opportunities are still there. But they are increasingly at the margins. It is not what today's broadcasting is about. Today's broadcasting is about winning. And that applies to the BBC as much as anywhere else.

There is nothing wrong with winning. Indeed, in an increasingly competitive system, winners are rightly at a premium. But a culture based largely on winning destroys the justification for the BBC as the necessary remedy for market failure. If winning is what we want, the market knows how to do that; sorting out winners and losers is what the market does in its sleep. Remedying market failure is about – well, failure. It is about deliberately failing to win large audiences, about deliberately failing to attract the right demographics, about not maximising the ratings in every slot. It is not caring too much about formats and secondary rights. It is about taking creative risks – and failing. It is, in an important sense, about socially and culturally desirable failure.

How can the BBC any longer be driven by such ambitions? Or indeed Channel 4. A mission statement, which declared as its main objective the intention to withdraw for social and cultural reasons from competition with rival broadcasters, would not be approved by either the BBC governors or the Channel 4 board. When there was only the BBC, ITV and Channel 4 on our televisions, no one talked about market failure. There weren't meaningful markets in programmes or airtime sales. The competition for audiences was real enough, but coming second or even third was not usually seen as a disaster.

Today, obviously, market competition is all pervasive in broadcasting. At 10am each working day meetings stop for anxious scrutiny of the overnight ratings. Neither the BBC nor Channel 4 wants to justify their existence as public service corporations in terms of market failure. And they are right to do so, in the sense that they are not going to attract the best talent if they go around with that label pinned to them.

The fundamental point is that the context in which our public service broadcasters operate has changed – and will continue to change – so profoundly that we will have to rethink what we mean by public service broadcasting, what we need it to do, what institutions can and should deliver it, and how it might be funded. There is no immediate crisis, but that doesn't really help. It can too easily lull an observer into thinking we can carry on as we are for the foreseeable future. And if we don't start thinking about it seriously now, we will increase the chances of not getting the right answers for the digital era. Fortunately the public debate that the government has initiated on reviewing the BBC Charter, together with the review of all public service broadcasting that Ofcom is required to carry out in 2004, offer an excellent opportunity to start serious thinking now.

Funding the BBC by voluntary subscriptions

This is where the 20-year-old Peacock vision should come back into consideration. Many of the problems posed by the existence of the BBC would disappear if its television services at least were funded by voluntary subscriptions rather than a compulsory licence fee. (This is not as radical a suggestion for a public service broadcaster as you might imagine. In Japan, the licence fee that funds NHK is effectively voluntary. I am told that about 90 per cent of people in the rural areas pay it, and 60 per cent of those in the cities.) The fair trading and competition issues that regularly provoke arguments between the BBC and its rivals would be substantially reduced, since it would be operating on fair terms in the pay TV market. The BBC would not need to get government approval for new services. Indeed its whole relationship with the government would be transformed for the better.

Of course some people would stop paying for the BBC. The BBC would have to manage the consequences of this, but that would do it no harm. As Channel 4 has discovered over the past three years, a downturn in your economic fortunes can offer a valuable opportunity to rethink your objectives and your structures. And much of the BBC's output no longer qualifies, in my view, for the 'merit good' justification – unlike our museums and galleries. Most of the programmes on BBC1 and BBC2 today are similar in kind and quality to those on ITV and Channel 4 (and indeed Channel 5). Few of them have a truly distinctive cultural and social value. In these circumstances I cannot see why we should not allow viewers to pay for the BBC voluntarily.

There are those who believe that the fact that pretty well everyone can get the BBC is one of its most important features. However, subscription needn't affect its universal availability – only whether people choose to take advantage of this availability.

Channel 4

In my view – and at this point let me insist that this is very much a personal view – the same applies to Channel 4. At the moment many of its programmes are, in a narrow sense, worth what the advertisers say they are worth. By a wonderful cultural accident, the original vision for Channel 4, as furnished by its first chief executive, Jeremy Isaacs, turned out to be a commercially very valuable one. That certainly wasn't Isaacs' intention – in his time Channel 4's income was secured by an impost on the revenues of the ITV companies, who sold the channel's airtime in their regions, thus preserving their commercial monopoly. Though the channel's income went up and down in step with the fortunes of ITV, the performance of its own programmes counted for little. Isaacs therefore embarked on a bold, innovative, minority-oriented, creatively risky strategy, with a schedule that defied usual commercial logic.

Of course much of this stuff did as a result fail commercially. It was the US comedy and drama imports that did the ratings trick. These were often bought jointly in a package with ITV, but were regarded by ITV as of insufficiently mainstream appeal, and cheerfully passed to the junior channel. Thus Channel 4 acquired what turned out to be a brilliant brand – for being different and adventurous (even though relatively few people actually watched the different and adventurous stuff) and cool – even though the cool was often imported American cool.

However, Channel 4 is now something of a prisoner of its brand and its success. The advertisers favoured it when it was separated from ITV for a number of reasons. One was simply relief at having somewhere other than ITV to go to. Another was the Channel's appeal to affluent light viewers and, increasingly, to young people – the 16 to 34s. These latter were – and are – highly desirable audiences because they spend generously on a wide range of products, but are very selective in their TV viewing and are therefore hard to reach. TV programmes that manage to reach them – and channels with youthful brand appeal – can therefore be sold to advertisers at a premium.

Unfortunately for Channel 4 many of the new channels that became available with the arrival of cable and satellite as serious competitors ten years ago spotted this, and went for the same audiences. Even ITV periodically tries to improve its appeal in this area. So Channel 4 has to concentrate more and more of its resources on programmes that serve this most valuable of audiences, ditching more and more of the old Isaacs-style programming as it does so. Tim Gardam, the Director of Programmes between 1999 and 2003, did a brilliant job of serving several different audiences, but it is hard to see any let-up in the relentless pressure to keep the 16–34 audiences at a significant level, whatever the consequences for the rest of the output.

Indeed some of the provisions of the Communications Act could make this pressure worse. Changes in the media ownership rules could allow Channel 5 to merge with either ITV or Sky. Either of these events would have adverse effects on Channel 4's airtime sales and its commissioning and purchasing of programmes. And the Carlton–Granada merger will certainly make all sales of airtime more difficult.

So these commercial pressures will intensify for as long as the main Channel 4 service relies entirely on advertising for its funding. One of the reasons for launching new services like E4 was to tap into pay TV revenues. However, as I explained in the previous chapter, the way the pay TV market is developing makes it unlikely that these revenues will add significantly to the channel's income. At some point the government might have to decide whether to preserve the channel's status as a public corporation and its current remit as a public service broadcaster, and if so whether to change the way it is funded. It could do this by providing it with public money – or find some other solution.

Retaining the BBC and Channel 4 as public corporations

I want to emphasise that I believe it is worth keeping both the BBC and Channel 4 as public corporations. Organisations that do not have shareholders and which cannot be taken over by private sector companies do have to work within the competitive programme-making cultures that I described earlier but, subject to that overall constraint, they can be more creatively ambitious, and take more and different kinds of risks than their private sector competitors. I believe the most important change the government could make for Channel 4 is to allow it, after digital switchover, to become a paid-for as well as advertising-funded service – if it wants to.

Channel 4 doesn't need to acquire the legitimacy that switching to subscription would, in my view, give the BBC; it already has that by virtue of its commercial independence. What pay revenues would offer is the chance to break the tyranny of the 16–34 demographic imperative. I suspect that many people who are older than 34 resent the fact that advertisers don't seem very interested in them, especially as one consequence is that we therefore find it harder to find programmes we want to watch on TV. With subscription we would have new economic power – the power of our willingness to pay to get the programmes we wanted.

I am not suggesting Channel 4 should give up its advertising revenues after digital switchover. There are two ways it could most obviously supplement these with pay TV income: through a premium service where its most expensive programming was shown first before going to the free service, and through a 'catch-up' service where people were able to pay to see programmes they had missed. Advertising would doubtless be its major source of income for many years – after all, only around 25 per cent of the revenues of the broadsheet papers comes from their cover price. The situation of the BBC is very different: we already pay for it, and in any change to subscription you would expect it to earn most of its money from this source.

Why make this change at switchover and not earlier? Because it is only when digital terrestrial television reaches its maximum audience that operating a near-universal terrestrial subscription service becomes feasible. At the same time privileged access to these near-universal channels may provide the basis for putting some kind of residual public service obligations on these organisations, even if they are partly funded by subscriptions.

What kind of public service objectives might need to be addressed in the free-market digital world that I am advocating? I think there are three main ones. First, we will need at least two competing high-quality, impartial news and current affairs services freely available to all. Second, subsidies to ensure that certain kinds of culturally and educationally valuable programmes or services can be made available either free or at an affordable price to those who wish to view them. Third, subsidies to make sure that those who live in remote areas have access to a minimum number of digital services. These objectives need to be considered separately, because they can be achieved by a number of different means; the funding of these means will almost certainly vary.

This is the profound challenge to the BBC. At the moment it is the beneficiary of two different subsidies. One (which it shares with Channel 4) is the free use of scarce spectrum – though this could change in future if and when the government chooses to bring these two networks fully within the new spectrum-charging regime that Ofcom is establishing. The other is its monopoly of the licence fee. How can such a monopoly survive if I am right about the three policy objectives for public funding in the digital world? We will need at least two competing news services, a range of different providers of subsidised cultural programmes and services, and subsidies to cope with problems created by geography. All this suggests the need for a variety of payment mechanisms, most directed to programmes and services, not institutions – and certainly not to just one institution.

Giving ourselves this kind of flexibility of objectives and funding is another argument for persuading – or forcing – the BBC to switch to subscription for its television services rather than continuing to be the sole beneficiary of the licence fee. It could – and doubtless would – get the benefit of some of the new public service broadcasting subsidies, but it would no longer be the main pillar of the system.

So far I have written solely about subscription as the new form of funding for the BBC. In fact that I think that at some point in the digital era it should be open to the BBC to sell advertising if it wanted to. In a conventional marketplace those offering products and services should be free to decide how they wanted to fund the production and distribution of these products and services. Just as ITV and Channels 4 and 5 should be able to charge for their output if they wanted to, so the BBC should be able to sell its airtime if it wanted to. However, such a radical change to the TV economy would certainly need phasing in, since it would have a very disruptive effect on the rest of broadcasting if introduced overnight.

Summary

We are approaching the 'near-perfect' market in television, which the former BBC chairman, Gavyn Davies, himself described as under-mining the case for the BBC in its current form. In such circum-stances the argument put by the Peacock Committee nearly 20 years ago for the abolition of the licence fee and its replacement by subscription seems to me overwhelming.

As a diverse, liberal democratic society we do not need the BBC as a secular Church of England, propagating a unifying cultural voice. Furthermore, the whole ethos of public service broadcasting, which includes ITV and Channel 4, is being undermined by the new, commercial values that dominate the creative culture in contemporary television.

I am under no illusion about the difficulty of getting such a policy adopted. The BBC is a formidable champion of its own cause. In Parliament, the Conservatives are beginning to question the licence fee. Opinion poll evidence on public support for the licence fee is unclear, and rather depends on who is asking the questions, though the growth of pay TV does seem to be beginning to undermine the public's support. Economic liberal newspapers – like *The Economist* and *Financial Times* – are opposed, as intermittently are the News International papers. The *Daily Mail* vehemently disliked the Dyke-led BBC. But the public is not – yet – in serious revolt against the licence fee; and I do not doubt that the BBC could organise a substantial middle England, middle-aged campaign in its defence that would put the efforts of the Countryside Alliance to shame.

Indeed, changing the funding and status of the BBC feels

comparable in magnitude to the task faced by the Protestant reformers in sixteenth-century England. The situation of the monasteries just prior to Dissolution has interesting, and not particularly comforting, parallels with the current position of the BBC. The monasteries had a comparable grip on culture. A minority of reformers loathed them, and criticised them vociferously, but the monasteries had the passive support of many, and the passionate loyalty of a substantial part of the population. When Henry VIII moved against them, he needed a minister with the rare abilities of Thomas Cromwell to lead the task; and he had to do it in stages. Even then the Dissolution provoked an armed revolt, which nearly cost Henry his throne. Ideology alone would not have been enough; it required the support of those landowners who stood to benefit substantially from the sale of the monastic lands and properties.

I am of course arguing for the reformation of the BBC, not its dissolution. However, I do not yet see any latter-day Thomas Cromwell in the ranks of New Labour interested in mounting an effective political assault on the BBC. Indeed, this prospect is perhaps now even more remote, given the public reaction to the turmoil at the BBC following the publication of the Hutton report. This does not, however, mean there might be no significant changes to the BBC as part of the Charter Review process that will be completed in 2006. This is the subject of the next chapter.

7. The BBC and Charter Review

A BBC funded by voluntary subscription is not practicable until the UK has completed the switch to digital television, because only then will a universally available encrypted terrestrial service be possible (programme services need to be encrypted to prevent those who haven't paid for them watching them for free). Most of the current Freeview set top boxes do not contain the conditional access system needed for pay services: the BBC took the strategic view that if it could create a sizeable universe of digital receivers that would only work with free to air services this would make it more difficult for any future government to abolish the licence fee. However, all integrated digital TV sets are required by European law to include conditional access, and these will in due course become the main consumer purchase.

The present BBC Charter runs out at the end of 2006. The government recently launched an ambitious consultation process, including pre-legislative scrutiny by Parliament, which is intended to deal comprehensively with all the issues affecting the BBC's future. By the end of 2005 the government hopes to have settled the arrangements for the BBC for the following ten years – the usual term for a new Charter. (The Culture Secretary, Tessa Jowell, has indicated that it is very unlikely the government would want to bring in a shorter term.)

So it is highly probable that the current funding system, of a compulsory licence fee, will run until the end of 2016. By that time Britain will almost certainly be well into the digital era: current government policy suggests that the terrestrial digital switchover programme should be completed between 2010 and 2012, though a firm decision on the timetable will not be made before the end of 2004 at the earliest.

However, the Charter Review process now under way will not only establish the extent and nature of public support for the licence fee in a multi-channel age; it could also lead to significant changes in the size, scope and organisation of the BBC even though the current funding arrangements remain essentially in place. The BBC could be much more tightly constrained, both by tighter remits on its services and by more effective external oversight. In many ways the current review is more threatening to the BBC than any in the past three decades.

It is also possible to imagine a radically different BBC, one with a new kind of public service purpose, and one more relevant to the digital environment. Ofcom's quest for a definition for 'public service broadcasting' will almost certainly have some bearing on the way the BBC's future role is defined. So in this final chapter I want to look at the most interesting potential outcomes, and assess their strategic significance for the BBC and public broadcasting.

Charter Review – the rival camps

The BBC battlefield is a complex and difficult terrain, occupied by a number of different forces whose differing objectives can sometimes be in conflict with and sometimes complement those of their rivals. On any one issue there can be an ad-hoc coalition of groups which on other matters are seriously opposed to each other. And what was an already complex situation was arguably made more so by the dramatic consequences of the publication of the Hutton report in January 2004, which led to the resignations of the chairman of the BBC, Gavyn Davies, and the director-general, Greg Dyke.

The episodes which prompted the Hutton inquiry themselves provide a good example of the complicated forces at work. People who wholeheartedly support the traditional idea of the BBC, but who were dismayed by what the David Kelly affair revealed about the state of some BBC journalism, united with others who believe the current governance of the BBC is hopelessly outdated, and that this was demonstrated in the way the governors mishandled the government's complaints about the *Today* journalist Andrew Gilligan. Both found themselves supported in their criticisms by some of those who dislike the very existence of a state-funded organisation like the BBC; though some of that group in turn preferred to defend the BBC on this occasion as a way of getting at the Blair government – the BBC in this instance being the lesser of two evils.

So, allowing for all the shifting alliances and nuances of attitude, here are what I believe are the main groups lining up to debate Charter Review.

o   *Loyal supporters of the status quo*
    These believe that any defects in the BBC are minor, and as nothing compared to the need to maintain the existence of a well-resourced, powerful public corporation that can face up to both commercial rivals and hostile governments.

o   *Disappointed traditionalists*
    These share the basic attitudes of the first group, but are much more concerned by what they see as 'dumbing down' at the BBC, and its much more aggressively commercial attitude to programming. They want the BBC to return to what they regard as proper public service values and performance.

o   *Proponents of the 'ghetto' BBC*
    These have a superficially similar analysis to the disappointed traditionalists, but start from a free market perspective rather than a public service one. Essentially, they want the BBC to abandon its wide-ranging ambitions (of providing all kinds of programmes in order to serve every section of the population) and to confine itself to

making those programmes that the commercial broadcasters can't or won't make.

○ *Defenders of commercial public service broadcasters*
To some extent these too share the view that the BBC has become too commercial, but their concern is with the impact of this on the ability of the advertising-funded channels, particularly ITV and Channel 4, to honour their PSB obligations. This camp can live with a slightly modified version of the current BBC provided there is an adequately funded public service competitor.

○ *Radical reformers (free market tendency)*
These think that the justification for any kind of licence fee-funded BBC is now past, though they have different emphases, depending on whether they primarily want a pure free market (privatising the BBC), a different form of public intervention (through, for example, 'contestable funding' – sometimes described as an 'arts council of the air'), or the continuation of a public corporation funded commercially with very limited privileges (for example, prominent display on electronic programme guides).

○ *Radical reformers (public service tendency)*
These share the view that technological change is challenging the whole basis of traditional public service broadcasting, but are more concerned to find new forms of public delivery that fit the world of broadband and the internet, multi-channel television and mobile handsets. They want to empower a new kind of active citizenship – which might or might not include retaining the BBC in some form.

Clearly no government could satisfy all these objectives. Tessa Jowell, the Secretary of State for Culture, Media and Sport, has already declared that 'the outcome of charter renewal will be a strong BBC and a BBC that is independent of government',[24] which closes off some of the more radical options for now. However, it leaves open the possibility of significant changes to the present arrangements. The test will be how far these go in adapting the BBC to the emerging digital world, and to what extent there is a vision of the long-term future into which such changes fit.

Tighter remits

For many years the commercial public service broadcasters have complained that while their obligations were tightly defined in their licences the BBC had only the vaguest of requirements in the Charter, and that this enabled the BBC to become more and more commercial in its programming (on BBC1 in particular), the more so as there was no external regulator to monitor and prevent such developments. One of the most blatant examples was the steady marginalisation of the main current affairs programme, *Panorama*, which over the years was moved from 8pm on Monday evenings to 10.15pm on Sundays. Similarly arts programmes almost disappeared from BBC1 for a few years until public criticism – and the approach of Charter Review – led to a change of policy in 2003.

The long-standing defence of the relative freedom given to the BBC by successive governments to interpret its PSB obligations (as compared to the tougher regime applied to ITV and Channel 4) was that it could be trusted to honour the spirit of the Charter. However, following the arrival of Greg Dyke as director-general in 2000 and the more commercially aggressive strategies he encouraged, this became visibly less tenable. The issue crystallised with the proposed launch of BBC3, a digital TV channel aimed at young people. There were strong objections to this from rival broadcasters who already transmitted services for precisely this audience, particularly from Channel 4, which had started its own version of such a channel, E4, in 2001. Much to the fury of the BBC, Tessa Jowell rejected the proposals for the new service on the grounds that they were insufficiently different from existing channels, and asked for a revised prospectus with a much stronger public service element. After a year of argument and public consultation, the BBC submitted new proposals. These were accepted by the DCMS – but the price paid by the BBC was a far more specific and detailed remit for the channel than had previously been imposed on any BBC service.

The BBC's critics have seized on this precedent. Giving the annual James MacTaggart Memorial Lecture at the Edinburgh TV Festival lecture in 2003, BSkyB chief executive Tony Ball argued that this kind of specific remit should exist for every BBC TV channel. It is hard to see a good argument against this proposal. It would meet some of the biggest concerns not only of the BBC's commercial rivals but of those I earlier called the disappointed traditionalists, who dislike the increasingly populist drift in BBC Television in recent years; and, unlike its response to some other suggested changes, the BBC has been noticeably quiet about this one.

It is politically and administratively easy to introduce such a change, and this is the most likely substantial reform to happen.

Reforming the BBC governors

Implicit in the situation described above is the suggestion of persistent failure by the BBC governors to hold the senior management to account, at least in the way the BBC's critics would like. It is one of the main reasons its rivals and competitors have long been arguing that there should be substantial reforms to the way the BBC is regulated. Most recently this has centred on the idea that the BBC should be brought fully under the new industry regulator, Ofcom, which took over the responsibilities of the old broadcasting regulators – the Independent Television Commission, Radio Authority, and Broadcasting Standards Commission – at the end of 2003.

Though it did give Ofcom some additional supervisory duties over the BBC's performance, the government accepted, during the parliamentary discussion of the Communications Bill, the BBC's argument that editorial policy should remain the province of the governors, not Ofcom. However, the justification for this special status was badly shaken just as the Bill was completing its legislative passage.

In the summer of 2003 a long-running row between the BBC and the government – its then communications director, Alastair

Campbell, in particular – over a report on the *Today* programme by defence correspondent Andrew Gilligan led to the suicide of Dr David Kelly. A government arms expert, he had been the main source for Gilligan's disputed story about the way intelligence material was used – or misused – to justify the invasion of Iraq.

As a result, the government set up the special inquiry by Lord Hutton to examine the circumstances surrounding Dr Kelly's suicide. One of the main issues was whether the BBC governors had properly investigated Campbell's complaints about the *Today* report. After a single three-hour meeting they had accepted the version of events provided by senior BBC managers, largely on the basis that they assumed the managers would have handled the matter adequately. In the event Lord Hutton ruled that key allegations in the original Gilligan broadcast were unfounded: that the BBC's supervisory editorial systems were defective; and that the governors had failed to look into the matter properly.

The Kelly affair highlighted in a particularly sombre manner the dilemma that the BBC governors have always had to live with: that they are both the champions of the BBC and the regulators who are supposed to hold it to account. On this occasion – understandably, given the excited atmosphere of the time and the deep divisions in Britain about the Iraq war – the governors had opted for the role of champions at the expense of their regulatory duties, and defended their journalists against what they saw as persistent and unjustified government pressure on the way the BBC was reporting the crisis. However, given that editorial mistakes were made, as the BBC subsequently conceded, the episode significantly reinforced the argument that the double role was no longer either appropriate or sustainable, and that changes to the governance of the BBC were now necessary.

Lord Hutton himself seemed to think that it would be possible for the governors to balance the potentially conflicting objectives of preserving the independence of the BBC while fulfilling the obligation to regulate the corporation properly and effectively. However, the history of the past twenty years suggests otherwise.

Twice now the governors have had to force the resignation of their directors-general – Alasdair Milne in 1987 and Greg Dyke in 2004. The long-serving chairman for much of this time, Lord Hussey, fell out not only with Milne but also with Milne's successors, Michael Checkland and – eventually – John Birt. In his much shorter tenure as chairman, Hussey's successor, Sir Christopher Bland, did appear to work well with both Birt and Dyke, but he had worked with them before and respected each for their very different qualities. (Bland's difficulties were with some of the other governors.) To my mind this suggests that the structural contradictions in the current arrangements not only lead to tensions with the outside world but are only manageable internally in the rare circumstances where chairman and director-general have a previous successful relationship on which they can build. Such a fortuitous combination is scarcely the basis for running a major institution like the BBC.

The issue has become whether this means putting the BBC fully under Ofcom, and turning the governors into non-executive board members (as is the case with Channel 4), or retaining the governors as a regulatory body but separated from the BBC, with its own staff and resources. The second might be the better alternative if it were linked to the next proposed change – diverting part of the BBC licence fee income to non-BBC purposes – since a new body (distinct from Ofcom) would then have a wider task.

Top-slicing the licence fee

The BBC has benefited greatly from the accident of timing which meant that the government awarded it a generous additional licence fee in 2000, to allow the BBC to follow its digital strategy of creating new specialist channels on both TV and radio plus a world-class internet presence, just before the dot.com bubble collapsed, and along with it TV advertising revenues.

Since 2001 the BBC's licence fee income has increased by more than 14 per cent while the advertising revenues of its main commercial competitor, ITV, have fallen by more than 6 per cent. The BBC has used some of this extra money to finance the digital channels, but it also significantly increased the budget for BBC1. In the same period BBC1's share of audience overtook ITV1 for the first time.

This has led to the suggestion that the BBC has too much money, an argument which has coincided with the revival in some quarters of the idea first espoused by the Peacock Committee in 1985: that in the era of multi-channel choice public intervention in the broadcasting market should, at least in part, be through public funding of a variety of channels, services and even individual programmes, and not just of the BBC (see chapters 1 and 6 above). It is an idea which Peacock labelled the 'Arts Council of the air', though some of its current proponents prefer the more contemporary title of 'contestable funding'. (This is expected to be one of the main recommendations of the Conservative Party's advisory committee on broadcasting, chaired by former Channel 5 chief executive David Elstein, which is due to report in February 2004.)

There are of course separate issues here. If it is felt that the BBC has too much money, this could be dealt with by reducing the licence fee, rather than handing a portion to others. If it is a good idea to create a new form of public funding in broadcasting this could come out of general taxation rather than the licence fee. And if some of the licence fee is reserved for other purposes these do not have to include subsidising the existing commercial broadcasters – it could be used for training, or for various kinds of community or local television.

Moreover, the concept of contestable funding divides the BBC's industry critics in a way that proposals to tighten the TV channel remits or reform the governors don't. It is condemned as bureaucratic, and unlikely to lead to the commissioning and broadcasting of good programmes (Channel 4, for example, is opposed to the idea, even though it might be supposed to be likely to benefit from it). Some people fear it would lead to less money overall being spent on original production. New Zealand has had such a body since 1990, with mixed results. In an article in the *Financial Times* in December 2003 the former Channel 4 director of television, Tim Gardam, reported that the New Zealand funding body had secured the continued production of many kinds of programmes that would otherwise have disappeared in the broadcasting free market that has existed there for a dozen years.[25] However since public funding was necessarily dependent on the broadcasters' willingness to transmit a funded programme, public money had on occasion gone to fund purely commercial material.

Other proposals

While the ideas discussed above are likely to be the main issues in the Charter Review debates, other proposals exist which would also result in significant changes to the traditional BBC. In his Edinburgh lecture Tony Ball argued that one of the BBC's most important public functions in future should be as a kind of creative incubator. It had the freedom to try out ideas and programmes that would be too risky for purely commercial operators. As and when these were successful, the BBC should auction them to be used by other broadcasters.

David Liddiment, the ITV network director of programmes between 1997 and 2002, has argued that the BBC programme production department should be able to make programmes for other broadcasters as well as the BBC, much in the way ITV companies like Granada are able to make programmes for the BBC. This links to wider concerns about the way the TV production market works in Britain, dominated as it is by the BBC and ITV with their in-house production capacities. Tony Cohen, the chief executive of Britain's biggest independent producer, Fremantle Media, has suggested that the BBC and ITV should be required to obtain at least half of the original production they broadcast from outside their own organisations. This goes well beyond the current requirement for 25 per cent of production to come from independent producers, and is an attempt to create a more genuinely free market in television production in this country.

A more radical kind of public service broadcasting

There is a very interesting new approach to delivering public services, which builds on changing technology to offer a new concept of how a publicly-funded resource can be exploited for public interest purposes. (Intriguingly, it has been, at least in part, embraced by the BBC itself.) It derives from the culture of the 'open source' movement that originated in the computer and IT worlds, and which still thrives there – for example, in the battle between Microsoft with its proprietary technologies and the supporters of Linux, the operating system which is an open standard. The fundamental principle of this movement is that as much information as possible should be freely shared.

The internet was created on this non-commercial basis; digital code wasn't encrypted, and anyone with the right expertise could use it as a building-block to improve on and make available to others. The basic language of the internet – HTML – is open. But the open source movement is not just about computer code: it is a value system, a cultural model.

The BBC identified itself with these values when its then director-general, Greg Dyke – giving the Richard Dunn Memorial Lecture at the Edinburgh International Television Festival in 2003 – announced that it would make the contents of its archives available to the public as long as the material was not re-used for commercial purposes. As Dyke said: 'It is not really (the BBC's) content – the people of Britain have paid for it and our role should be to help them use it.'[26]

The BBC has had discussions with the leading American exponent of open source ideas, Lawrence Lessig, a law professor at Stanford University. Lessig advocates the introduction of new intellectual property laws that protect digital information from piracy but which do not also lead to the erosion of the public's right to share and use it on a non-commercial basis. He argues that the current climate of copyright restrictions is leading to a situation where creativity itself is being adversely affected.[27]

In the same lecture, Dyke added: 'I believe we are about to move into a second phase of the digital revolution, a phase that will be more about public than private value.' It remains unclear whether this was the announcement of a new strategic direction for the BBC, or was closer to a public relations tactic. But either way, Dyke's announcement of the creative archive made a direct appeal to our residual feelings for the BBC as a unique cultural asset.

A variant on this idea was put forward by Patricia Hodgson, the chief executive of the former Independent Television Commission, in her *New Statesman* Lecture in the autumn of 2003 when she called for the creation of a 'BBC Public Trust' to meet what she described as the 'global appetite for the best of Britain's intellectual capital'. The Trust, she said, would have 'a duty to exploit the UK's intellectual property for those theatres, museums, universities and orchestras which wish to benefit from the scale, connections and promotional power of the BBC', using its formidable international profile.[28]

There is much that is attractive about what Lessig calls a 'Creative Commons'. (Lessig is also adapting this approach to the way the radio spectrum is used – a 'Spectrum Commons'.) However, it clearly conflicts not just with the commercial imperatives of big and small media organisations, but with the ambitions of writers, journalists and programme makers who want to make their fortunes out of their creative productions. It is hard to believe they would want to allow their efforts to enter the public domain on this basis until most of the commercial value had been squeezed from them – which in some cases could be decades away. Nonetheless, it is possible to imagine a smaller, more purely public service-oriented BBC, which could indeed operate on this basis.

Conclusion

Even without the fallout from Hutton, the government and the BBC would have faced a very difficult strategic dilemma over the BBC's future which both of them would have tried to ignore. However, irrespective of what either of them might do now, they know that the digital revolution, and the speed with which consumers are changing the ways in which they use television, will make it very difficult to retain the current status and funding of the BBC once switchover happens. Both are likely to be tempted to make as small a change as possible now, though the government might be willing to go further than the BBC would like. However, the reaction to Hutton may further reduce their appetite for radical change (such as top-slicing the licence fee), since the government will want to avoid any suggestion of vindictiveness. Nonetheless, the long-term choice remains between a big BBC funded commercially and a much smaller one funded largely by public money.

This choice can be ducked for now, but successors to the present regimes will not have this luxury. The fundamental contradictions in the BBC's status – that people are forced to pay for one particular media service when they have ever-increasing freedom of choice in every other instance, and the existence of a monolithic state organisation which has such a damaging impact on legitimate commercial activity – will become more and more intolerable. If the BBC does not at some point take the initiative itself, a future government will start to cut the licence fee – and once started the process will be difficult to reverse.

In one sense, the imaginative BBC move to open up its archive to free public use could be seen as a slightly cynical attempt to re-position itself in the new world without sacrificing any of its present power. Whatever the motivation behind this initiative, it is difficult to see that an organisation of more than 20,000 people can easily cohere for long around both aggressive commercial values (reaching maximum audiences, optimising secondary revenues) and the public-spirited ethos of the open source movement. The BBC will have to choose where its heart lies. Does it want to be big or does it want to do good?

The whole argument of this booklet is that it would be better for the rest of us if we had a big BBC which earned its living commercially, but it would not be a disaster if the BBC shrank to being a new kind of public service institution. Under the second scenario, many talented people would leave the BBC to work – and often, I suspect, prosper – in the larger commercial sector – if that still existed.

This brings me to the second main theme of this pamphlet: that the monopolistic character of the current British pay TV market is as much in need of reform as the BBC. We are spending billions of pounds as individual consumers on material for our TV screens – but much of this material originates outside the UK. Not because the foreign producers are better than ours, but because ours can't get to our wallets as easily. The historically successful British programme production industry has been, and largely remains, cut off from dealing directly with the people who watch or use its products. If we want to see our creative talent flourish in the new world, and if as viewers we want in the digital era the same range of well-made British programmes that we have enjoyed for the past 50 years, then we must remove the structural barriers that currently prevent the normal way we go shopping for what we want from working in the context of television. ITV and Channel 4 should be free to charge us to watch *Coronation Street* or *Wife Swap* if they want to; and Sky should be stopped from making us pay for channels we don't want in order to get those we do.

Ofcom has many duties, but its main ones are to further the interests of both consumers and citizens. Both are served by the existence of a high-quality, large-scale UK TV production industry equipped to satisfy the widest possible range of tastes and interests. But this industry will be a smaller, weaker thing if its main customers are a diminished BBC and a few freesheet channels. Substantial social, cultural and economic issues are involved in the move to a fully digital world. If governments and regulators do nothing, we will – as consumers – eventually decide the outcomes by our behaviour. However, public policy should have a real place in affecting the outcome; so it would be better if, as citizens, we encouraged governments and regulators to reach the right policy and the right results sooner rather than later.

References

1. BBC Annual Report 2002; ITC, *The UK Televisions Market: An Overview*, September 2003.
2. A Peacock et al, *Report of the Committee on Financing the BBC* (HMSO, 1986).
3. G Davies, *The Future Funding of the BBC* (DCMS, 1999).
4. ITC, *Multichannel Quarterly*, second quarter 2003.
5. BSkyB press release, 'Results for the three months ended 30 September 2003', 14 November 2003.
6. Ofcom, *Internet and Broadband Update*, January 2004.
7. According to a speech by Sir Christopher Bland, Chairman, BT Group plc at the FT Media and Broadcasting Conference, 5 March 2002.
8. Available to download from http://www.doh.gov.uk/newsdesk/archive/june2001/4-naa-28062001.html.
9. ITC, *The UK Televisions Market: An Overview*, September 2003.
10. Entertainment and Leisure Software Publishers' Association (ELSPA) press release, 'Video Games Continue to Grow', 6 January 2003 – see www.elspa.com.
11. British Video Association Yearbook 2003, http://www.bva.org.uk/yearbook.asp.
12. B Macleod, 'Just get your act together', *Financial Times*, 10 September 2002.
13. Source: Channel 4.
14. J Cassy, 'This is the new internet', *Guardian*, 23 September 2002.
15. World Administrative Radio Conference 1977 (WARC-77).
16. BSkyB press release, 'Sky reaches seven million subscriber target early', 1 October 2003.
17. Sky Annual Reports 2002, 2003.
18. BT press release, 'BT micropayment service makes it easier to Click&Buy™ online', 24 April 2002.
19. A Peacock et al, *Report of the Committee on Financing the BBC*.
20. G Davies, *The Future Funding of the BBC*.
21. Ibid.

22. In a speech given to the Emmy Board, New York, 24 November 2003 – the full text is available at http://www.bbc.co.uk/pressoffice/speeches/stories/dyke_emmy.shtml.
23. *New Statesman*, 30 September 2002.
24. In an interview with David Frost on BBC1's *Breakfast with Frost*, 1 February 2004.
25. T Gardam, 'Television – Lessons in culture from down', *Financial Times*, 23 December 2003.
26. Full text available on the BBC website, at http://www.bbc.co.uk/pressoffice/speeches/stories/dyke_richard_dunn.shtml.
27. See www.creativecommons.org.
28. P Hodgson, *Has TV got news for you? – Government, business and regulation*, The *New Statesman* lecture, 15 October 2003 – the full text is available at http://www.newstatesman.com/pdf/itc2004supp.pdf.

DEMOS – Licence to Publish

THE WORK (AS DEFINED BELOW) IS PROVIDED UNDER THE TERMS OF THIS LICENCE ("LICENCE"). THE WORK IS PROTECTED BY COPYRIGHT AND/OR OTHER APPLICABLE LAW. ANY USE OF THE WORK OTHER THAN AS AUTHORIZED UNDER THIS LICENCE IS PROHIBITED. BY EXERCISING ANY RIGHTS TO THE WORK PROVIDED HERE, YOU ACCEPT AND AGREE TO BE BOUND BY THE TERMS OF THIS LICENCE. DEMOS GRANTS YOU THE RIGHTS CONTAINED HERE IN CONSIDERATION OF YOUR ACCEPTANCE OF SUCH TERMS AND CONDITIONS.

1. **Definitions**
   a **"Collective Work"** means a work, such as a periodical issue, anthology or encyclopedia, in which the Work in its entirety in unmodified form, along with a number of other contributions, constituting separate and independent works in themselves, are assembled into a collective whole. A work that constitutes a Collective Work will not be considered a Derivative Work (as defined below) for the purposes of this Licence.
   b **"Derivative Work"** means a work based upon the Work or upon the Work and other pre-existing works, such as a musical arrangement, dramatization, fictionalization, motion picture version, sound recording, art reproduction, abridgment, condensation, or any other form in which the Work may be recast, transformed, or adapted, except that a work that constitutes a Collective Work or a translation from English into another language will not be considered a Derivative Work for the purpose of this Licence.
   c **"Licensor"** means the individual or entity that offers the Work under the terms of this Licence.
   d **"Original Author"** means the individual or entity who created the Work.
   e **"Work"** means the copyrightable work of authorship offered under the terms of this Licence.
   f **"You"** means an individual or entity exercising rights under this Licence who has not previously violated the terms of this Licence with respect to the Work, or who has received express permission from DEMOS to exercise rights under this Licence despite a previous violation.
2. **Fair Use Rights.** Nothing in this licence is intended to reduce, limit, or restrict any rights arising from fair use, first sale or other limitations on the exclusive rights of the copyright owner under copyright law or other applicable laws.
3. **Licence Grant.** Subject to the terms and conditions of this Licence, Licensor hereby grants You a worldwide, royalty-free, non-exclusive, perpetual (for the duration of the applicable copyright) licence to exercise the rights in the Work as stated below:
   a to reproduce the Work, to incorporate the Work into one or more Collective Works, and to reproduce the Work as incorporated in the Collective Works;
   b to distribute copies or phonorecords of, display publicly, perform publicly, and perform publicly by means of a digital audio transmission the Work including as incorporated in Collective Works;
   The above rights may be exercised in all media and formats whether now known or hereafter devised. The above rights include the right to make such modifications as are technically necessary to exercise the rights in other media and formats. All rights not expressly granted by Licensor are hereby reserved.
4. **Restrictions.** The licence granted in Section 3 above is expressly made subject to and limited by the following restrictions:
   a You may distribute, publicly display, publicly perform, or publicly digitally perform the Work only under the terms of this Licence, and You must include a copy of, or the Uniform Resource Identifier for, this Licence with every copy or phonorecord of the Work You distribute, publicly display, publicly perform, or publicly digitally perform. You may not offer or impose any terms on the Work that alter or restrict the terms of this Licence or the recipients' exercise of the rights granted hereunder. You may not sublicence the Work. You must keep intact all notices that refer to this Licence and to the disclaimer of warranties. You may not distribute, publicly display, publicly perform, or publicly digitally perform the Work with any technological measures that control access or use of the Work in a manner inconsistent with the terms of this Licence Agreement. The above applies to the Work as incorporated in a Collective Work, but this does not require the Collective Work apart from the Work itself to be made subject to the terms of this Licence. If You create a Collective Work, upon notice from any Licencor You must, to the extent practicable, remove from the Collective Work any reference to such Licensor or the Original Author, as requested.
   b You may not exercise any of the rights granted to You in Section 3 above in any manner that is primarily intended for or directed toward commercial advantage or private monetary

compensation. The exchange of the Work for other copyrighted works by means of digital file-sharing or otherwise shall not be considered to be intended for or directed toward commercial advantage or private monetary compensation, provided there is no payment of any monetary compensation in connection with the exchange of copyrighted works.

c If you distribute, publicly display, publicly perform, or publicly digitally perform the Work or any Collective Works, You must keep intact all copyright notices for the Work and give the Original Author credit reasonable to the medium or means You are utilizing by conveying the name (or pseudonym if applicable) of the Original Author if supplied; the title of the Work if supplied. Such credit may be implemented in any reasonable manner; provided, however, that in the case of a Collective Work, at a minimum such credit will appear where any other comparable authorship credit appears and in a manner at least as prominent as such other comparable authorship credit.

5. Representations, Warranties and Disclaimer

  a By offering the Work for public release under this Licence, Licensor represents and warrants that, to the best of Licensor's knowledge after reasonable inquiry:

   i Licensor has secured all rights in the Work necessary to grant the licence rights hereunder and to permit the lawful exercise of the rights granted hereunder without You having any obligation to pay any royalties, compulsory licence fees, residuals or any other payments;

   ii The Work does not infringe the copyright, trademark, publicity rights, common law rights or any other right of any third party or constitute defamation, invasion of privacy or other tortious injury to any third party.

  b EXCEPT AS EXPRESSLY STATED IN THIS LICENCE OR OTHERWISE AGREED IN WRITING OR REQUIRED BY APPLICABLE LAW, THE WORK IS LICENCED ON AN "AS IS" BASIS, WITHOUT WARRANTIES OF ANY KIND, EITHER EXPRESS OR IMPLIED INCLUDING, WITHOUT LIMITATION, ANY WARRANTIES REGARDING THE CONTENTS OR ACCURACY OF THE WORK.

6. Limitation on Liability. EXCEPT TO THE EXTENT REQUIRED BY APPLICABLE LAW, AND EXCEPT FOR DAMAGES ARISING FROM LIABILITY TO A THIRD PARTY RESULTING FROM BREACH OF THE WARRANTIES IN SECTION 5, IN NO EVENT WILL LICENSOR BE LIABLE TO YOU ON ANY LEGAL THEORY FOR ANY SPECIAL, INCIDENTAL, CONSEQUENTIAL, PUNITIVE OR EXEMPLARY DAMAGES ARISING OUT OF THIS LICENCE OR THE USE OF THE WORK, EVEN IF LICENSOR HAS BEEN ADVISED OF THE POSSIBILITY OF SUCH DAMAGES.

7. Termination

  a This Licence and the rights granted hereunder will terminate automatically upon any breach by You of the terms of this Licence. Individuals or entities who have received Collective Works from You under this Licence, however, will not have their licences terminated provided such individuals or entities remain in full compliance with those licences. Sections 1, 2, 5, 6, 7, and 8 will survive any termination of this Licence.

  b Subject to the above terms and conditions, the licence granted here is perpetual (for the duration of the applicable copyright in the Work). Notwithstanding the above, Licensor reserves the right to release the Work under different licence terms or to stop distributing the Work at any time; provided, however that any such election will not serve to withdraw this Licence (or any other licence that has been, or is required to be, granted under the terms of this Licence), and this Licence will continue in full force and effect unless terminated as stated above.

8. Miscellaneous

  a Each time You distribute or publicly digitally perform the Work or a Collective Work, DEMOS offers to the recipient a licence to the Work on the same terms and conditions as the licence granted to You under this Licence.

  b If any provision of this Licence is invalid or unenforceable under applicable law, it shall not affect the validity or enforceability of the remainder of the terms of this Licence, and without further action by the parties to this agreement, such provision shall be reformed to the minimum extent necessary to make such provision valid and enforceable.

  c No term or provision of this Licence shall be deemed waived and no breach consented to unless such waiver or consent shall be in writing and signed by the party to be charged with such waiver or consent.

  d This Licence constitutes the entire agreement between the parties with respect to the Work licensed here. There are no understandings, agreements or representations with respect to the Work not specified here. Licensor shall not be bound by any additional provisions that may appear in any communication from You. This Licence may not be modified without the mutual written agreement of DEMOS and You.